W9-BVH-652

chemo caps & wraps™

Contents

Give a halo of hope

Cancer is a life-changing illness. It changes the lives of those who are diagnosed, as well as the lives of the family and friends of the cancer patient. In this day and age, there's hardly anyone whose life has not been touched by cancer in some way.

My life changed when my late husband was diagnosed with cancer at the early age of 21. Even though almost 30 years have passed since his death, I still vividly remember the kindness and support of friends and family, as well as the hundreds of cards from people I did not even know.

In *Chemo Caps & Wraps*, you will find projects that will help you make a difference in the life of a cancer patient, whether that person is a friend, family member or someone you don't even know. All of the caps have been designed with the chemo patient in mind and are designed to fit over the patient's entire head. The yarns used are soft, in order to avoid irritating the scalp, which is sensitive during the chemo process. In addition to caps, we've also included beautiful wraps for the patient to use while waiting for a doctor's visit or during treatments. As cancer knows no boundaries, caps and wraps for babies and children have also been included.

Cancer does indeed change lives, a fact that Pamela Haschke knows firsthand. After enduring a dose-dense chemotherapy regimen for the treatment of inflammatory breast cancer, Pamela decided she would give back. With the full support of family and friends, as well as gifts of handmade caps and wraps, she founded Halos of Hope, a not-for-profit organization that sends hats for chemo patients all over the United States. A portion of the proceeds from each *Chemo Caps & Wraps* book sold will be donated to Halos of Hope. More information about Halos of Hope can be found on page 3.

Please take this opportunity to show someone you care by stitching a handmade cap or wrap, and don't forget to donate to your local hospital or cancer center.

Make a difference!

Connie

Halos of Hope

"Cancer is a journey of courage.
Let us embrace you along the way."

Halos of Hope began after Pamela Haschke endured a dose-dense chemotherapy regimen for treatment of inflammatory breast cancer. During her treatment, Pam received numerous hats and scarves from friends and family who created these items to cover her balding head. After she left treatment and began her arduous trek to recovery, Ms. Haschke decided to give back in order to help others who might suffer from the embarrassing and painful effects of hair loss.

Invited to attend the inaugural LIVESTRONG Summit sponsored by the Lance Armstrong Foundation, she reached out to friends and family, and started a grassroots movement to provide cancer caps to oncology offices and hospitals in her area. Word soon spread and the requests for caps multiplied. She heeded the call and recruited every willing volunteer from a growing list of states and sent the additional hats to more centers and hospitals. She enlisted the help of a colleague to form Halos of Hope as a not-for-profit 501c3 organization. In two short years, this grassroots movement has become a national organization that has helped thousands across the country. Using grants and donations, Halos now has hats shipped from a not-for-profit distribution center to an ever-growing list of oncology offices, hospitals and cancer centers around the country.

By the end of 2009, Halos of Hope's handcrafted hats found their way to over 150 centers in 39 states, and requests continue to pour in. While no cap request is ever denied, Halos tries to ensure the centers in our most-challenged communities regularly receive hats, as these populations are often overlooked. Each hat goes to its center with a tag attached "Cap created by a Halos of Hope Volunteer."

At the end of 2009, Halos of Hope was selected by the American Society for Radiation Oncology (ASTRO), as a Survivor Circle partner. ASTRO selects only 2 charities per year for this distinction.

Halos of Hope is an all-volunteer organization with no paid staff, and its board accepts no compensation.

A key objective for 2010 is to find as many local yarn shops or other local craft businesses that would be willing to serve as drop-off points for hats in their communities. If you would like to become a drop-off point, make a donation or have a hat request, information is below.

Halos of Hope
P.O. Box 1998
Arlington Heights, IL 60006-1998
info@halosofhope.org

If you are associated with a cancer center that needs hats, please send an e-mail to info@halosofhope.org with your center's information, or enter the information on the "Contact Us" page at www.halosofhope.org.

Halos of Hope maintains an online Web site for monetary donations. For other donations such as yarn, needles and supplies, please contact info@halosofhope.org before sending.

4

Kelly

Currently undergoing chemotherapy for colon cancer

Summer Sorbet
Cap & Wrap

DESIGNS BY **EDIE ECKMAN**

SKILL LEVEL

EASY

FINISHED SIZE

Cap: Instructions given fit most children and women

FINISHED MEASUREMENTS

Cap: 22½-inch circumference

Wrap: Approx 14 x 50 inches

MATERIALS

- Plymouth Yarns Fantasy Naturale medium (worsted) weight yarn (3½ oz/140 yds/100g per hank):
  Cap: 1 hank #9878
  Wrap: 4 hanks #9878
- Size H/8/5mm crochet hook or size needed to obtain gauge

GAUGE

Wrap and Cap: 12 sc = 5 inches
Cap: Rnds 1 and 2 = 3 inches in diameter

PATTERN NOTES

Join with slip stitch unless otherwise stated.

Chain-3 at beginning of row or round counts as first double crochet unless otherwise stated.

SPECIAL STITCHES

Extended double crochet (ext dc): Yo, insert hook in indicated st or sp, draw lp through, yo, draw through 1 lp, (yo, draw through 2 lps) twice.

Beginning cluster (beg cl): Ext dc *(see Special Stitches)* in st or sp indicated, dc between double strand formed at base of ext dc.

Cluster (cl): Ext dc in st or sp indicated, 2 dc between double strand formed at base of ext dc.

INSTRUCTIONS

CAP

Rnd 1: Ch 4, **join** *(see Pattern Notes)* in 4th ch from hook to form ring, **ch 3** *(see Pattern Notes)*, 11 dc in ring, join in top of beg ch-3. *(12 dc)*

Rnd 2: Ch 3, **beg cl** *(see Special Stitches)* in first ch of beg ch-3, **cl** *(see Special Stitches)* in each st around, join in top of beg ch-3. *(12 cl)*

Note: All cl after this point are worked into the sp between 2 cl.

Rnd 3: Ch 3, beg cl in sp before first cl of previous rnd, *cl in next sp, 2 cl in next sp**, cl in next sp, rep from * around, ending last rep at **, join in top of beg ch-3. *(16 cl)*

Rnds 4 & 5: Ch 3, beg cl in sp before first cl of previous rnd, cl in each rem sp around, join in top of beg ch-3.

Rnd 6: Ch 3, beg cl in sp before first cl of previous rnd, *2 cl in next sp**, cl in next sp, rep from * around, ending last rep at **, join in top of beg ch-3. *(24 cl)*

Rnds 7–11: Ch 3, beg cl in sp before first cl of previous rnd, cl in each sp around, join in top of beg ch-3.

Rnd 12: Ch 1, sc in same st as beg ch-1, sc in next st, sk next st, *sc in each of next 2 sts, sk next st, rep from * around, join in first sc. *(48 sc)*

Rnds 13–16: Ch 1, sc in each st around, join in first sc. Fasten off at end of last rnd.

Weave in ends.

WRAP

Row 1: Ch 44, sc in 2nd ch from hook and in each ch across, turn. *(43 sc)*

Rows 2–5: Ch 1, sc in each st across, turn.

Row 6: Ch 3 *(see Pattern Notes)*, *sk next 2 sc, **cl** *(see Special Stitches)* in next sc, rep from * across, turn. *(14 cl)*

Note: All cl after this point are worked into the sp between 2 cl.

Row 7: Ch 3, cl in each sp between cl across, placing last cl in sp between last cl and beg ch-3, turn.

Rep Row 7 until piece measures approximately 48 inches from beg.

Next row: Ch 1, sc in each st across, turn. *(43 sc)*

Next rows: Rep rows 2–5. Fasten off at end of last row. Weave in ends. ■

Austin

Paternal and maternal grandparents are cancer survivors

Just for Him

DESIGN BY **MARGARET HUBERT**

SKILL LEVEL

EASY

FINISHED SIZE
One size fits most

FINISHED MEASUREMENT
Approx 22-inch circumference

MATERIALS
- Berroco Comfort medium (worsted) weight yarn (3½ oz/210 yds/100g per ball):
    1 ball #9713 dusk
- Size K/10½/6.5mm crochet hook or size needed to obtain gauge

GAUGE
12 sc = 4 inches; 16 rows = 4 inches

PATTERN NOTE
Work rows 1–31 in **back loops** (*see Stitch Guide*) unless otherwise stated.

INSTRUCTIONS
HAT
Foundation row: Ch 67, sc in 2nd ch from hook and in each rem ch across, turn. (*66 sc*)

Row 1 (RS): Ch 1, working in **back lps** (*see Pattern Note*), sc in each sc across, turn.

Rows 2–22: Rep row 1.

Row 23 (RS): Ch 1, sc in each of next 4 sc, **sc dec** (*see Stitch Guide*) in next 2 sts, *sc in each of next 6 sc, sc dec in next 2 sts, rep from * 6 times, sc in each of last 4 sc, turn. (*58 sc*)

Row 24 (WS): Rep row 1.

Row 25: Ch 1, sc in each of next 3 sc, sc dec in next 2 sts, *sc in each of next 5 sc, sc dec in next 2 sts, rep from * 6 times, sc in each of last 4 sc, turn. (*50 sc*)

Row 26: Rep row 1.

Row 27: Ch 1, sc in each of next 3 sc, sc dec in next 2 sts, *sc in each of next 4 sts, sc dec in next 2 sts, rep from * 6 times, sc in each of last 3 sc, turn. (*42 sc*)

Row 28: Rep row 1.

Row 29: Ch 1, sc in each of next 2 sts, sc dec in next 2 sts, *sc in each of next 3 sc, sc dec in next 2 sts, rep from * 6 times, sc in each of last 3 sts, turn. (*34 sc*)

Row 30: Rep row 1.

Row 31: Ch 1, *sc dec in next 2 sts, rep from * across. (*17 sc*)

Fasten off, leaving a 36-inch length for finishing.

FINISHING
Using a tapestry needle and rem length, gather rem 17 sc, and pull tight, rep gather once. Using the same yarn, sew back seam, matching ridges as you sew. Weave in ends. ■

Cable Cap & Lapghan

DESIGNS BY **ROSALIE JOHNSTON**

SKILL LEVEL

INTERMEDIATE

FINISHED SIZE
Cap: Instructions given fit most

FINISHED MEASUREMENTS
Cap: Approx 7½ inches long x 24-inch circumference

Lapghan: 30 x 40 inches

MATERIALS
- Caron Simply Soft medium (worsted) weight (3 oz/157 yds/85g per skein:
  Cap: 1 skein #2721 autumn red
  Lapghan: 8 skeins #2721 autumn red
- Size I/9/5.5mm crochet hook or size needed to obtain gauge

GAUGE
6 hdc = 2 inches; 6 rows = 2 inches

PATTERN NOTES
Chain-2 does not count as a stitch unless otherwise stated.

Skip stitch behind each front post treble crochet unless otherwise stated.

Rosalie

Crochet designer—
Mother is a breast cancer
survivor

My 84-year-old mother had surgery for breast cancer, and most likely will not need chemo, but her diagnosis did make me think about all of the younger women losing their hair while receiving cancer treatments. I would love to be part of a crochet project that could possibly help them with their self-image during their treatment.

To change length of Cap, stitches may be added in any number. Change stitches in middle of row, keeping 4 half double crochet before cable and keeping 6 unworked half double crochet at end of indicated rows. If changing number of stitches, be sure to change stitch count at end of rows in instructions.

To change circumference of Cap, add or subtract rows in multiples of 4. Pattern must end with row 5.

To change the width of the Lapghan, stitches can be added in multiples of 6. As an example, work 13 stitches instead of 12 stitches between cables. This would result in an increase of 6 stitches and 2 inches in width (from 34 to 36 inches).

To change the length of the Lapghan, add or subtract rows in multiples of 4. Pattern must end with row 7. Then work row 120 to finish.

SPECIAL STITCHES

Front post treble crochet (fptr): Yo twice, insert hook from front to back around post of indicated st, yo and pull up a lp even with st on hook, (yo and draw through 2 lps on hook) 3 times.

Backward single crochet (backward sc): Holding yarn in front, insert hook from the back to front in indicated st and draw lp through to back, yo, draw through 2 lps on hook.

INSTRUCTIONS

CAP

Row 1 (RS): Leaving a 6-inch tail, ch 27, hdc in 3rd ch from hook and in each rem ch across, turn. (25 hdc)

*Note: Work all rem even-numbered rows in both lps and all rem odd-numbered rows in **back lps** (see Stitch Guide) unless otherwise stated.*

Row 2: Ch 2 (see Pattern Notes), hdc in first hdc and in each rem hdc across, turn. (25 hdc)

Row 3: Ch 2, hdc in each of next 4 hdc, **fptr** (see Special Stitch) around each of next 3 hdc 1 row below, **sk hdc behind each fptr** (see Pattern

Notes), hdc in each of next 12 hdc, leaving last 6 hdc unworked, turn. (19 sts)

Row 4: Ch 1, sk first hdc, hdc in each rem st across, turn. (18 hdc)

Row 5: Ch 2, hdc in each of first 4 hdc, sk next fptr, fptr around each of next 2 fptr, working in front of the 2 fptr just made, fptr around sk fptr, hdc in each of next 11 hdc, hdc in next ch, hdc in same back lp as last hdc 2 rows below, hdc dec in next 2 hdc 2 rows below, hdc in each of last 4 hdc 2 rows below, turn. (25 sts)

Row 6: Ch 2, hdc in each st across, turn.

Row 7: Ch 2, hdc each of first 4 sts, fptr around each of next 3 fptr, hdc in each of next 12 hdc, leave last 6 hdc unworked, turn. (19 sts)

Rows 8–63: [Rep rows 4–7 consecutively] 14 times.

Rows 64 & 65: Rep rows 4 and 5.

Leaving 20-inch tail for sewing, fasten off.

FINISHING

With WS facing, weave tail through sts at top of Cap (side opposite of cable), and pull tight to gather. Sew 1 st through other side (row 65) to join. To secure, tie knot with working yarn and tail rem from row 1. Using rem 20-inch tail, sew seam down side of Cap, making sure to match up ends of cables. Weave in loose ends.

LAPGHAN

Row 1 (RS): Ch 107, hdc in 3rd ch and in each ch across, turn. (105 hdc)

*Note: Work all rem even rows in both lps and all rem odd rows in **back lps** (see Stitch Guide) unless otherwise stated.*

Row 2: Ch 2, hdc in each hdc across, turn. (105 hdc)

Row 3: Ch 2, working in **back lps** (see Note, hdc in each of next 6 hdc, *fptr (see Special Stitch) around each of next 3 hdc 1 row below, **sk hdc**

Row 4: Ch 2, hdc in each hdc across, turn. (105 hdc)

Row 5: Ch 2, hdc in each of first 6 hdc, *sk next fptr, fptr around each of next 2 fptr, working in front of 2 fptr just made, fptr around sk fptr**, hdc in each of next 12 hdc, rep from * across, ending last rep at **, hdc in each of next 6 hdc, turn.

Row 6: Ch 2, hdc in each hdc across, turn. (105 hdc)

Row 7: Ch 2, hdc in each of first 6 hdc, *fptr around each of next 3 fptr**, hdc in each of next 12 hdc, rep from * across, ending last rep at **, hdc in each of next 6 hdc, turn.

Rows 8–119: [Rep rows 4–7 consecutively] 28 times. *Note: For Option 2 only, fasten off at end of last row. Do not turn.*

OPTION 1
Row 120 (WS): Ch 1, working in both lps, **backward sc** *(see Special Stitches)* in each st across. Fasten off and weave in ends.

OPTION 2
Row 120: Join in first st of row 119, ch 1, working in both lps, sc in each st across. Fasten off and weave in ends. ∎

behind each fptr *(see Pattern Notes)***, hdc in each of next 12 hdc, rep from * across, ending last rep at **, hdc in each of last 6 hdc, turn. (105 sts)

Dot

Breast cancer survivor—4 years

Flower Shawl & Cap

DESIGNS BY **MARGARET HUBERT**

SHAWL

SKILL LEVEL

EASY

FINISHED MEASUREMENT
Approx 76 inches wide across top

MATERIALS
- Berroco Comfort medium (worsted) weight yarn (3½ oz/210 yds/100g per ball):
    4 balls # 9705 pretty pink
    1 ball #9740 seedling
- Sizes H/8/5mm and I/9/5.5mm crochet hooks or size needed to obtain gauge

GAUGE
Size I hook: 3 ch-5 sps and 4 sc = 4 inches

PATTERN NOTES
Chain-9 counts as first double crochet and chain-5 unless otherwise stated.

Join with slip stitch unless otherwise stated.

INSTRUCTIONS
SHAWL
Row 1: With size I hook and pretty pink, ch 10, **join** (see Pattern Notes) in first ch to form ring, **ch 9** (see Pattern Notes), sc in ring, ch 5, dc in ring, turn. (2 ch-5 sps made)

Row 2: Ch 9, sc in next ch-5 sp, *ch 5, sc in next ch-5 sp, ch 5, dc in 3rd ch of the beg ch-9, turn. *(3 ch-5 sps)*

Row 3: Ch 9, sc in first ch-5 sp, *ch 5, sc in next ch-5 sp, rep from * once, ch 5, dc in the 3rd ch of beg ch-9 sp, turn. *(4 ch-5 sps)*

Row 4: Ch 9, sc in first ch-5 sp, *ch 5, sc in next ch-5 sp, rep from * twice, ch 5, dc in 3rd ch of beg ch-9, turn. *(5 ch-5 sps)*

Rows 5–55: Ch 9, sc in first ch-5 sp, *ch 5, sc in next ch-5 sp, rep from * across to beg ch-9, ch 5, dc in 3rd ch of beg ch-9. Fasten off. *(57 ch-5 sps at end of last row)*

FLOWER
MAKE 9.

Rnd 1: With size H hook and pretty pink, ch 4, **join** *(see Pattern Notes)* in 4th ch from hook to form ring, ch 1, 10 sc in ring, join in beg ch-1.

Rnd 2: *Ch 3, 5 dc in next st, ch 3 sl st in next st, rep from * 4 times more, join in base of beg ch-3. Fasten off, leaving an 18-inch length of yarn for sewing to Shawl. *(5 petals)*

FLOWER CENTER

Using seedling, work a **French knot** *(see illustration)* in center of Flower. Work Flower Center in center of each rem Flower.

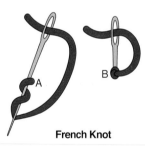

French Knot

LEAF
MAKE 9.

With size H hook and seedling, ch 14, dc in 5th ch from hook and in each of next 3 chs, hdc in each of next 3 chs, sc in each of next 3 chs, ch 3, working on opposite side of beg ch-14, sc in each of first 3 chs, hdc in each of next 3 chs, dc in each of next 4 chs, ch 3, join in same ch as last dc. Leaving an 18-inch length of yarn for sewing, fasten off.

FRINGE

Cut 3 strands, each 8 inches long. Fold strands in half, pull fold through sp, pull ends through fold. Pull to tighten.

Fringe around dc or ch-6 sp at end of each row and in beg ch-10. *(111 Fringe)*

FINISHING
Pin Flowers and Leaves in place as shown in Placement Diagram.

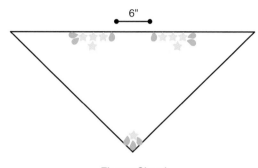

Flower Shawl
Placement Diagram

Using rem 18-inch lengths, sew Flowers and Leaves in place.

CAP

SKILL LEVEL

EASY

FINISHED SIZE
One size fits most

FINISHED MEASUREMENT
Approx 21-inch circumference

MATERIALS
- Berroco Comfort medium (worsted) weight yarn (3½ oz/210 yds/100g per ball):
  2 balls #9705 pretty pink
  1 ball #9740 seedling
- Sizes H/8/5mm and I/9/5.5mm crochet hooks or size needed to obtain gauge
- Stitch marker

GAUGE
Size I hook: 14 sc = 4 inches; 16 rows = 4 inches

PATTERN NOTES
Cap is worked in continuous rounds.

Do not join at end of each round.

Use stitch marker to mark end of each round. Move marker as work progresses.

Join with slip stitch unless otherwise stated.

INSTRUCTIONS
CAP

Rnd 1: With pretty pink, beg at center top of Cap, ch 4, **join** (*see Pattern Notes*) in 4th ch from hook to form ring, ch 1, 8 sc in ring, **do not join** (*see Pattern Notes*), **place marker** (*see Pattern Notes*).

Rnd 2: 2 sc in each sc around. (*16 sc*)

Rnd 3: [Sc in first sc, 2 sc in next sc] around. (*24 sc*)

Rnd 4: [Sc in each of next 2 sc, 2 sc in next sc] around. (*32 sc*)

Rnd 5: [Sc in each of next 3 sc, 2 sc in next sc] around. (*40 sc*)

Rnd 6: [Sc in each of next 4 sc, 2 sc in next sc] around. (*48 sc*)

Rnd 7: [Sc in each of next 5 sc, 2 sc in next sc] around. (*56 sc*)

Rnd 8: [Sc in each of next 6 sc, 2 sc in next sc] around. (*64 sc*)

Rnd 9: [Sc in each of the next 7 sc, 2 sc in next sc] around. (*72 sc*)

Rnds 10–24: Sc in each sc around.

Rnd 25: Sc in each sc around, join in first sc.

Rnd 26: Ch 4 (*counts as a dc, ch-1*), sk next sc, [dc in next st, ch 1, sk next st] around, join in 3rd ch of beg ch-4. (*36 dc, 36 ch-1 sps*)

Rnd 27: Ch 1, *sc in next ch-1 sp, sc in next dc, rep from * 34 times, sc in next ch-1 sp, join in beg ch-1.

Rnd 28: Ch 1, *sc in each of next 3 sc, 2 sc in next sc, rep from * 17 times, join in beg ch-1. (*90 sc*)

Rnd 29: Ch 1, sc in each sc around, join in beg ch-1.

Rnds 30–34: Rep rnd 29.

Rnd 35: Ch 1, **reverse sc** (*see illustration*) in each sc around. Fasten off.

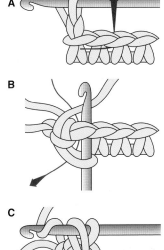
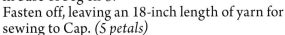

Reverse Single Crochet

FLOWER
MAKE 10.

Rnd 1: With size H hook and pretty pink, ch 4, **join** (*see Pattern Notes*) in 4th ch from hook to form ring, ch 1, 10 sc in ring, join in beg ch-1.

Rnd 2: *Ch 3, 5 dc in next st, ch 3 sl st in next st, rep from * 4 times more, join in base of beg ch-3. Fasten off, leaving an 18-inch length of yarn for sewing to Cap. (*5 petals*)

FLOWER CENTER

Using seedling, work a **French knot** (*see illustration*) in center of Flower. Work Flower Center in center of each rem Flower.

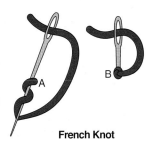

French Knot

LEAF
MAKE 3.

With size H hook and seedling, ch 14, dc in 5th ch from hook and in each of next 3 chs, hdc in each of next 3 chs, sc in each of next 3 chs, ch 3, working on opposite side of beg ch-14, sc in each of first 3 chs, hdc in each of next 3 chs, dc in each of next 4 chs, ch 3, **join** (*see Pattern Notes*) in same ch as last dc. Leaving an 18-inch length of yarn for sewing, fasten off.

FINISHING

Following Placement Diagram, pin Flowers end to end around rnd 26 of Cap. Using rem 18-inch lengths, sew each Flower to Cap. ■

Flower Cap
Placement Diagram

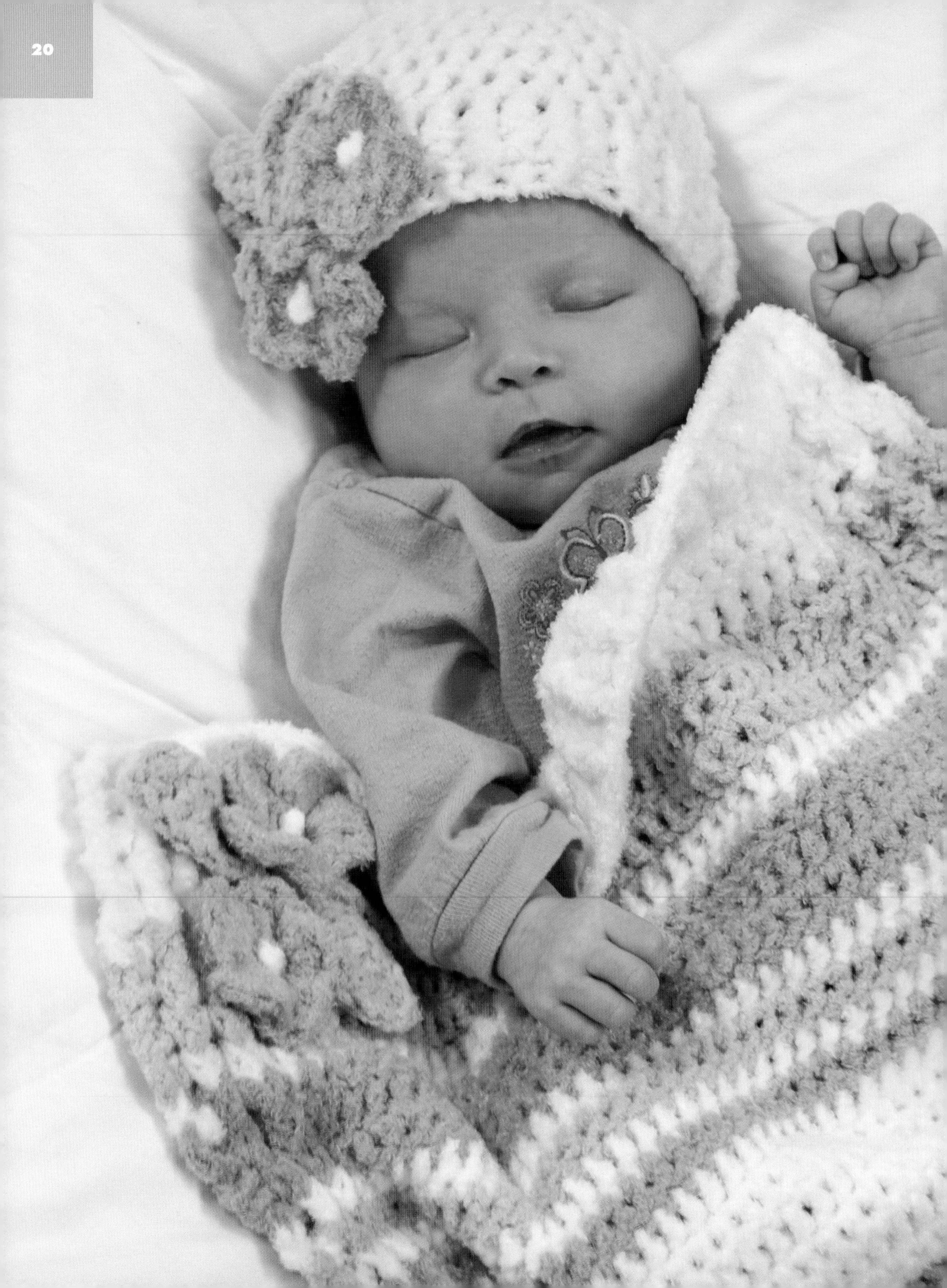

Cassie

Grandmother died from colon cancer

Bitty Baby Cap & Wrap

DESIGNS BY **FRANCES HUGHES**

SKILL LEVEL
■■□□
EASY

FINISHED SIZE
Cap: Instructions given fit infant's small; changes for medium and large are in [ ].

Wrap: Instructions given for small; changes for medium and large are in [ ].

FINISHED MEASUREMENTS
Cap: 10- [12½-, 15-] inch circumference

Wrap: 12¼ [14¾, 17¼] x 20 [30, 32] inches

MATERIALS
- Plymouth Yarn Oh My! bulky (chunky) weight yarn (1¾ oz/70 yards/50g per ball):
  5 [5, 6] balls #12 yellow
  2 [2, 3] balls each #54 pink and #19 green
- Size F/5/3.75mm crochet hook or size needed to obtain gauge

GAUGE
4 sts = 1 inch; 2 rows = 1 inch

PATTERN NOTE
Join with slip stitch unless otherwise stated.

INSTRUCTIONS

CAP
Rnd 1: With yellow, ch 4, **join** (see Pattern Note) in first ch to form a ring, ch 3, 9 dc in ring, join in top of beg ch-3. (10 dc)

Rnd 2: Ch 3, dc in same dc as beg ch-3, 2 dc in each dc around, join in top of beg ch-3. (20 dc)

Rnd 3: Ch 3, dc in same dc as beg ch-3, dc in next dc, [2 dc in next dc, dc in next dc] around, join in top of beg ch-3. (30 dc)

Rnd 4: Ch 3, dc in same dc as beg ch-3, dc in each of next 2 dc, [2 dc in next dc, dc in each of next 2 dc] around, join in top of beg ch-3.

SIZES MEDIUM & LARGE ONLY
Rnd [5]: Ch 3, dc in same dc as beg ch-3, dc in each of next 3 dc, [2 dc in next dc, dc in each of next 3 dc] around, join in top of beg ch-3. (50 dc)

SIZE LARGE ONLY
Rnd [6]: Ch 3, dc in same dc as beg ch-3, dc in each of next 4 dc, [2 dc in next dc, dc in each of next 4 dc] around, join in top of beg ch-3. (60 dc)

ALL SIZES
Rnds 5–9 [6–10, 7–11]: Ch 3, dc in each dc around, join in top of beg ch-3. (40 [50, 60] dc)

EDGING RIB
Rnds 10 & 11 [11 & 12, 12 & 13]: Ch 3, **bpdc** (see Stitch Guide) around next dc, [**fpdc** (see Stitch Guide) around next dc, bpdc around next dc] around, join in top of beg ch-3. Fasten off.

WRAP
Row 1: With yellow, ch 52 [62, 72], dc in 4th ch from hook and in each rem ch across, turn.

Row 2: Ch 3, **bpdc** (see Stitch Guide) around next dc, [**fpdc** (see Stitch Guide) around next dc, bpdc around next dc] across, turn.

Row 3: Ch 3, bpdc around next dc, [fpdc around next dc, bpdc around next dc] across, turn.

Row 4: Ch 3, [fpdc around next fpdc, bpdc around next bpdc] twice, dc in each dc across to last 5 sts, [fpdc around next fpdc, bpdc around next bpdc] twice, dc in top of beg ch-3.

Row(s) 5 [5 & 6, 5–7]: Rep row 4, **changing color** (see Stitch Guide) to green at end of row.

Rows 6–8 [7–10, 8–12]: With green, rep row 4, changing color to yellow at end of last row.

Row(s) 9 [11 & 12, 13 & 14]: With yellow, rep row 4, changing color to pink at end of row.

Rows 10–12 [13–16, 15–18]: With pink, rep row 4, changing color to yellow at end of last row.

Row(s) 13 [17 & 18, 19 & 20]: With yellow, rep row 4, changing color to green at end of row.

Row(s) 14 [19 & 20, 21 & 22]: With green, rep row 4, changing color to yellow at end of row.

Row(s) 15 [21 & 22, 23 & 24]: With yellow, rep row 4, changing color to pink at end of row.

Row(s) 16 [23 & 24, 25 & 26]: With pink, rep row 4, changing color to yellow at end of row.

Rows 17–24 [25–36, 27–38]: With yellow, rep row 4, changing color to pink at end of last row.

Row(s) 25 [37 & 38, 39 & 40]: With pink, rep row 4, changing color to yellow at end of row.

Row(s) 26 [39 & 40, 41 & 42]: With yellow, rep row 4, changing color to green at end of row.

Row(s) 27 [41 & 42, 43 & 44]: With green, rep row 4, changing color to yellow at end of row.

Row(s) 28 [43 & 44, 45 & 46]: With yellow, rep row 4, changing color to pink at end of row.

Rows 29–31 [45–48, 47–50]: With pink, rep row 4, changing color to yellow at end of last row.

Row(s) 32 [49 & 50, 51 & 52]: With yellow, rep row 4, changing color to green at end of row.

Rows 33–35 [51–54, 53–57]: With green, rep row 4, changing color to yellow at end of last row.

Rows 36 & 37 [55–57, 58–60]: With yellow, rep row 4.

Rows 38–40 [58–60, 61–64]: Rep row 3. Fasten off at end of last row.

FLOWER
MAKE 5.
Rnd 1: With pink, ch 3, **join** (see Pattern Note) in first ch to form ring, ch 1, 5 sc in ring.

Rnd 2: (Sc, 3 dc, sc) in each sc around. Fasten off.

FLOWER CENTER
Using green, work a **French knot** (see illustration) in center of Flower. Work Flower Center in center of each rem Flower.

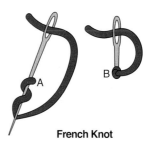

French Knot

LEAF
MAKE 5.
With green, ch 8, sc in 2nd ch from hook, hdc in next ch, dc in each of next 3 chs, hdc in next ch, 4 sc in last ch, working on opposite side of ch, hdc in next ch, dc in each of next 3 chs, hdc in next ch, sc in last ch, **join** (see Pattern Note) in beg sc. Fasten off. Place 3 Flowers and 2 Leaves on Cap, and 2 Flowers and 3 Leaves on Wrap as shown in photo. ∎

Infusion Wrap

DESIGN BY **NANCY NEHRING**

SKILL LEVEL

INTERMEDIATE

FINISHED SIZES

Instructions given fit 30–32-inch circumference (*small*); changes for 34–36-inch circumference (*medium*), 38–40-inch circumference (*large*), 42–44-inch circumference (*X-large*) and 46–48-inch circumference (*2X-large*) are in [ ].

FINISHED GARMENT MEASUREMENTS

Chest: 38 [44, 49, 53, 59] inches

MATERIALS

- Plymouth Yarn Dreambaby DK light (DK) weight yarn (1¾ oz/183 yds/ 50g per ball):
    9 [11, 12, 13, 15] balls #136 blue
- Size H/8/5mm crochet hook or size needed to obtain gauge
- Stitch markers
- 1¼–1½-inch buttons: 12
- Sewing needle
- Thread
- 1½-inch wide grosgrain ribbon: 36 inches (optional)
- Straight pins (optional)

GAUGE

12 sts = 4 inches; 13 rows = 4 inches

PATTERN NOTES

When deciding which instructions to use, use the measurement that has the largest circumference, i.e. bust/chest, waist or hip.

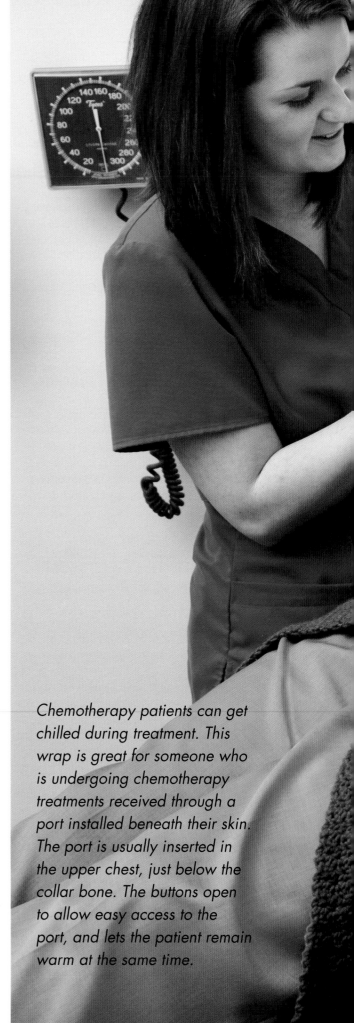

Chemotherapy patients can get chilled during treatment. This wrap is great for someone who is undergoing chemotherapy treatments received through a port installed beneath their skin. The port is usually inserted in the upper chest, just below the collar bone. The buttons open to allow easy access to the port, and lets the patient remain warm at the same time.

Timberly
Grandfather died from cancer

Tony
Physician Assistant who works with
cancer patients and their families

Yarn amounts are given for a person 5 feet 4 inches tall. Add or subtract approximately 1 skein for each 4 inches that recipient is taller or shorter. Finished wrap should fall below knee.

If intended recipient is shorter or taller than 5 feet 4 inches, add or subtract rows in 13-row increments.

Chain-2 at beginning of row counts as first single crochet unless otherwise stated.

Chain-3 at beginning of row counts as first double crochet unless otherwise stated.

Join with slip stitch unless otherwise stated.

INSTRUCTIONS
FIRST YOKE
BOTTOM
Row 1: Ch 59 [67, 75, 81, 89], sc in 3rd ch from hook *(first 2 chs count as sc)*, [sc in next ch, dc in next ch] across, turn. *(58 [66, 74, 80, 88] sts)*

Row 2: Ch 2 *(see Pattern Notes)*, sk same st as beg ch-2, [dc in next sc, sc in next dc] across to last st, dc in top of beg 2 sk chs, turn.

Rows 3 & 4: Ch 2, sk same st as beg ch-2, [dc in next sc, sc in next dc] across to last st, dc in top of beg ch-2, turn.

BUTTONHOLES
SECTION 1
SIZES SMALL, MEDIUM, LARGE & 2X-LARGE ONLY
Row 5: Ch 2, sk same st as beg ch-2, [dc in next sc, sc in next dc] 2 [2, 2, 3] times, leaving rem sts unworked, turn.

Row 6: Ch 3 *(see Pattern Notes)*, sk same st as beg ch-3, [sc in next dc, dc in next sc] across, turn.

Row 7: Ch 2, sk same st as beg ch-2, [dc in next sc, sc in next dc] across. Fasten off.

SIZE X-LARGE ONLY
Row [5]: Ch 2, sk same st as beg ch-2, [dc in next sc, sc in next dc] [twice], dc in next st, leaving rem sts unworked, turn.

Rows [6 & 7]: Ch 2, sk same st as beg ch-2, [dc in next sc, sc in next dc] across to last st, dc in last st, turn. Fasten off at end of last row.

SECTION 2
SIZES SMALL, MEDIUM, LARGE & 2X-LARGE ONLY
Row 5: Join *(see Pattern Notes)* in next sk st on row 4, ch 3, sk same st as beg ch-3, [sc in next dc, dc in next sc] 4 [5, 6, 7] times, leaving rem sts unworked, turn.

Row 6: Ch 2, sk same st as beg ch-2, [dc in next sc, sc in next dc] across, turn.

Row 7: Ch 3, sk same st as beg ch-3, [sc in next dc, dc in next sc] across. Fasten off.

SIZE X-LARGE ONLY
Row [5]: Join *(see Pattern Notes)* in next sk st on row 4, ch 2, sk same st as beg ch-2, [dc in next sc, sc in next dc] [6] times, dc in next st, leaving rem sts unworked, turn.

Rows [6 & 7]: Ch 2, sk same st as beg ch-2, [dc in next sc, sc in next dc] across to last st, dc in last st, turn. Fasten off at end of last row.

SECTION 3
SIZES SMALL, MEDIUM & X-LARGE ONLY
Row 5: Join in next sk st on row 4, ch 2, sk same st as beg ch-2, [dc in next sc, sc in next dc] 4 [5, 6] times, dc in next st, leaving rem sts unworked, turn.

Rows 6 & 7: Ch 2, sk same st as beg ch-2, [dc in next sc, sc in next dc] across to last st, dc in last st, leaving rem sts unworked, turn. Fasten off at end of last row.

SIZES LARGE & 2X-LARGE ONLY
Row [5]: Join in next sk st on row 4, ch 2, sk same st as beg ch-2, [dc in next st, sc in next dc] [6, 7] times, leaving rem sts unworked, turn.

Row [6]: Ch 3, sk same st as beg ch-3, [sc in next dc, dc in next sc] across, turn.

Row [7]: Ch 2, sk same st as beg ch-2, [dc in next st, sc in next dc] across. Fasten off.

SECTION 4
SIZES SMALL, MEDIUM & X-LARGE ONLY
Row 5: Join in next sk st on row 4, ch 2, sk same st as beg ch-2, [dc in next sc, sc in next dc] 4 [4, 5] times, dc in next st, leaving rem sts unworked, turn.

Rows 6 & 7: Ch 2, sk same st as beg ch-2, [dc in next sc, sc in next dc] across to last st, dc in last st, turn. Fasten off at end of last row.

SIZES LARGE & 2X-LARGE ONLY
Row [5]: Join in next sk st on row 4, ch 3, sk same st as beg ch-3, [sc in next dc, dc in next sc] [5, 6] times, sc in next st, leaving rem sts unworked, turn.

Rows [6 & 7]: Ch 3, sk same st as beg ch-3, [sc in next dc, dc in next sc] [5, 6] times, sc in last st, turn. Fasten off at end of last row.

SECTION 5
SIZES SMALL, MEDIUM & X-LARGE ONLY
Rep Section 3 for these sizes.

SIZES LARGE & 2X-LARGE ONLY
Rep Section 2 for these sizes.

SECTION 6
SIZES SMALL & MEDIUM ONLY
Row 5: Join in next sk st on row 4, ch 2, sk same st as beg ch-2, [dc in next st, sc in next dc] 4 [5] times, leaving rem sts unworked, turn.

Row 6: Ch 3, sk same st as beg ch-3, [sc in next dc, dc in next sc] across, turn.

Row 7: Ch 2, sk same st as beg ch-2, [dc in next st, sc in next dc] across. Fasten off.

SIZES LARGE & 2X-LARGE ONLY
Rep Section 3 for these sizes.

SIZE X-LARGE ONLY
Rep Section 2 for this size.

SECTION 7
SIZES SMALL, MEDIUM, LARGE & 2X-LARGE ONLY
Row 5: Join in next sk st, ch 3, sk same st as beg ch-3, [sc in next dc, dc in next sc] 2 [2, 2, 3] times, turn.

Row 6: Ch 3, sk same st as beg ch-3, [sc in next dc, dc in next sc] across, turn.

Row 7: Ch 2, sk same st as beg ch-2, [dc in next sc, sc in next dc] across. **Do not fasten off.**

SIZE X-LARGE ONLY
Row [5]: Join in next sk st, ch 2, sk same st as beg ch-2, [dc in next sc, sc in next dc] [twice], dc in next st, turn.

Rows [6 & 7]: Ch 2, sk same st as beg ch-2, [dc in next sc, sc in next dc] [twice], dc in next st, turn. **Do not fasten off** at end of last row.

CHEST
ALL SIZES
Row 8: Working across all sections, ch 2, sk same st as beg ch-2, [dc in next sc, sc in next dc] across to last st in last section, dc in last st, turn. *(58 [66, 74, 80, 88] sts)*

Rows 9–20: Ch 2, sk same st as beg ch-2, [dc in next sc, sc in next dc] across to last st, dc in last st, turn. Fasten off at end of last row. Mark last st of last row.

2ND YOKE
Rep First Yoke. **Do not fasten off** at end of row 20.

CHEST & SHOULDER
Row 21: Ch 2, sk same st as beg ch-2, [dc in next sc, sc in next dc] across to last 15 sts, dc in next st, leaving rem sts unworked, turn. *(44 [52, 60, 66, 74] sts)*

Rows 22–46: Ch 2, sk same st as beg ch-2, [dc in next sc, sc in next dc] across to last st, dc in last st, turn. Fasten off at end of last row. Mark last st of last row.

FIRST YOKE CONTINUED
SHOULDER
Row 21: Sk first 14 sts to left of marker, join in next st, ch 2, sk same st as beg ch-2, [dc in next sc, sc in next dc] across to last st, dc in last st, turn. *(44 [52, 60, 66, 74] sts)*

Rows 22–46: Ch 2, sk same st as beg ch-2, [dc in next sc, sc in next dc] across to last st, dc in last st, turn.

BACK

Row 47: Ch 2, sk same st as beg ch-2, [dc in next sc, sc in next dc] across to last st, dc in last st, ch 28, join with sc in marked st in row 46 of 2nd Yoke, dc in next sc, sc in next dc across to last st, dc in last st, turn. *(88 [104, 120, 132, 148] sts, 1 ch-28 sp)*

Row 48: Ch 2, sk same st as beg ch-2, [dc in next sc, sc in next dc] across to last st before ch 28, dc in last st, [sc in next ch, dc in next ch] across ch 28, [sc in next dc, dc in next sc] across rem sts, turn. *(116 [132, 148, 160, 176] sts)*

Rows 49–80: Ch 2, [dc in next sc, sc in next dc] across to last st, dc in last st, turn. Fasten off at end of last row.

LOWER BODY

Row 1: Ch 29 [33, 37, 40, 44], sk first 29 [33, 37, 40, 44] sts of Back, join with dc in next sc on Back, [sc in next dc, dc in next sc] 29 [33, 37, 40, 44] times, sc in next dc, ch 30 [34, 38, 42, 46], leaving rem sts unworked, turn.

Row 2: Dc in 3rd ch from hook *(first 2 chs count as sc)*, [sc in next ch, dc in next ch] across to last ch, sc in last ch, working across sts from row 1, [dc in next sc, sc in next dc] across to ch 29 [33, 37, 40, 44], [dc in next ch, sc in next ch] across to last ch, dc in last ch, turn. *(116 [132, 148, 160, 176] sts)*

Rows 3–91: Ch 2, sk same st as beg ch-2, [dc in next sc, sc in next dc] across to last st, dc in last st, turn. Fasten off at end of last row.

BACK LEFT BUTTON FLAP

Row 1: Join in first st of row 80 of Back, ch 2, sc in each sk st across to beg of Lower Body, turn. *(29 [33, 37, 40, 44] sts)*

Rows 2–12: Ch 2, sc in each sc across, turn. Fasten off at end of last row.

BACK RIGHT BUTTON FLAP

Row 1: Join yarn in first sk st of 2nd group of sk sts in row 80 of Back, ch 2, sc in each sk st across to end of row 80, turn. *(29 [33, 37, 40, 44] sts)*

Rows 2–12: Ch 2, sc in each sc across, turn. Fasten off at end of last row.

LOWER BODY LEFT BUTTON FLAP

Row 1: Working in rem lps of row 1 of Lower Body, join yarn in rem lp of row 1 opposite first st of row 2 of Lower Body, sc in each of next 29 [33, 37, 40, 44] sts, turn.

Rows 2–12: Ch 2, sc in each sc across, turn. Fasten off at end of last row.

LOWER BODY RIGHT BUTTON FLAP

Row 1: Working in rem lps of row 1 of Lower Body, join yarn in rem lp of row 1 opposite 87th [99th, 111th, 120th, 132nd] st of row 2 of Lower Body, sc in each rem st across, turn.

Rows 2–12: Ch 2, sc in each sc across, turn. Fasten off at end of last row.

NECK EDGING

With yarn taut, measure 68 inches of yarn, leave a little for ends, cut and tie into a circle. Flatten circle so yarn is double stranded.

Row 1: With RS of Wrap facing, hold 1 end of double-stranded circle against back of row 20 of 2nd Yoke, join yarn in first sc of row 20 of 2nd Yoke, making sure to insert hook through end of yarn circle, ch 2, now working over both strands of yarn circle, sc in each of next 14 sts, working in ends of rows, sc evenly sp across row 47 of Back, sc in each sc across to edge of row 46 of First Yoke Shoulder, sc in end of each row across to row 20 of First Yoke, sc in each sk st across to last st of row 20 of First Yoke, sc in last sk st on row 20 of First Yoke, making sure to insert hook through rem end of yarn circle, turn.

Rows 2–3: Ch 2, sc in each of next 13 sts, sk next 2 sts, sc in each of next 24 sts, sk next 2 sts, sc in each of next 26 sts, sk next 2 sts, sc in each of next 24 sts, sk next 2 sts, sc in each of last 13 sts, turn. Fasten off at end of last rnd.

FOLDING

Fold Wrap as shown in Folding Diagram. Fold Button Flaps up or down to overlap Back and Lower Body.

BUTTON ATTACHMENT

Position buttons on Button Flaps adjacent to
Buttonholes. Sew buttons to Button Flaps.

BUTTON ATTACHMENT OPTION

Instead of sewing buttons to Button Flaps, use
straight pins to pin buttons in place. If desired,
cut twelve 1¼ x 1½-inch squares of ribbon and
sew ribbon behind each pinned button. Sew
buttons to Button Flaps and to ribbon. ■

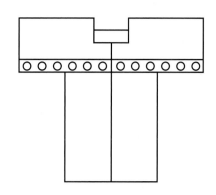

Infusion Wrap
Folded

KEY
– – – Fold
●●● Button Flap

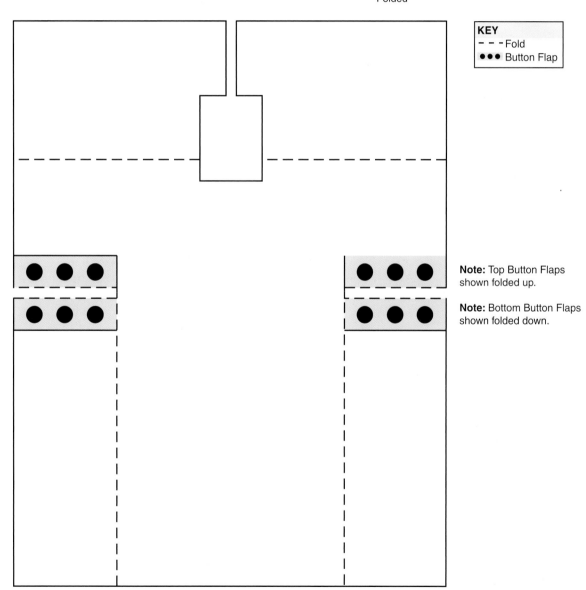

Note: Top Button Flaps
shown folded up.

Note: Bottom Button Flaps
shown folded down.

Infusion Wrap
Folding and Button Flap
Placement Diagram

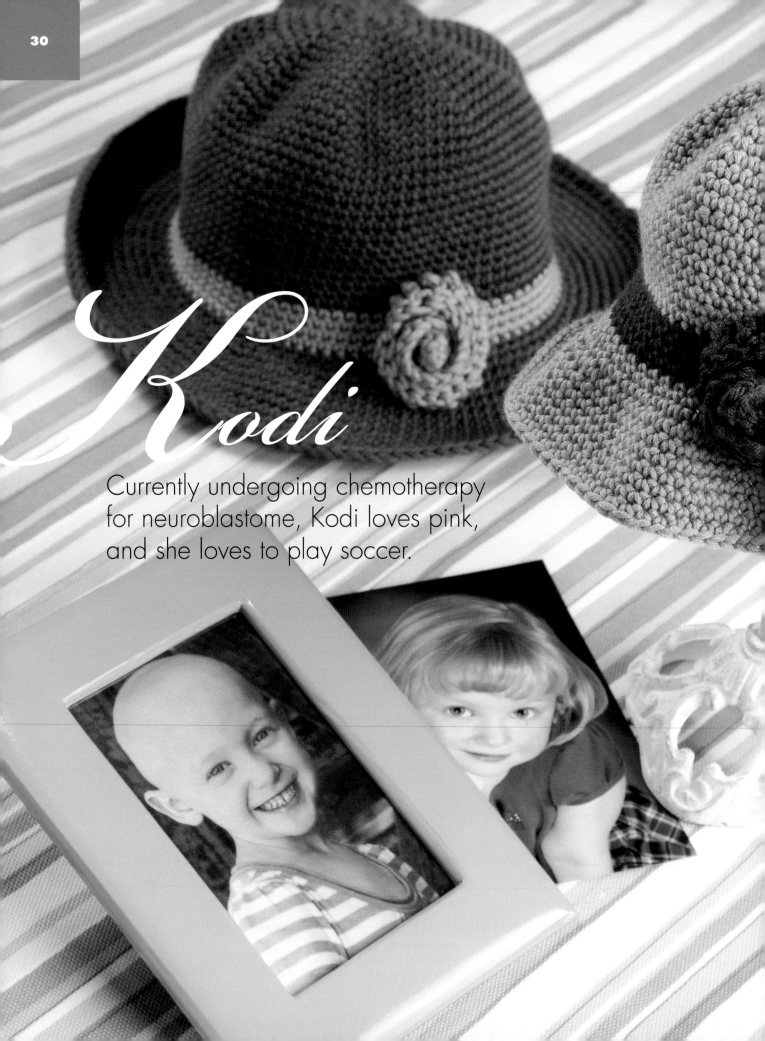

Kodi

Currently undergoing chemotherapy
for neuroblastome, Kodi loves pink,
and she loves to play soccer.

Adult's & Child's
Floppy Hats

DESIGNS BY **BECKY STEVENS**

ADULT'S FLOPPY HAT

SKILL LEVEL

EASY

FINISHED SIZE
One size fits most

FINISHED MEASUREMENT
Approx 21½-inch circumference

MATERIALS
- Berroco Comfort medium (worsted) weight yarn (3½ oz/210 yds/100g per ball):
    2 balls #9794 wild raspberry heather *(MC)*
    1 ball #9728 raspberry sorbet *(CC)*
- Size G/6/4mm hook or size needed to obtain gauge
- Stitch markers
- Safety pin

GAUGE
5 sc = 1 inch; 4 sc rnds = 1 inch

PATTERN NOTES
Hat is worked in continuous rounds.

Do not join or turn unless otherwise stated.

Place marker at end of each round to mark beginning of following round. Move marker as each round is completed.

INSTRUCTIONS
ADULT'S HAT

Rnd 1: With MC, ch 4, sl st in 4th ch from hook to form ring, ch 1, work 10 sc in ring, **place marker** *(see Pattern Notes)*. *(10 sc)*

Rnd 2: 2 sc in each sc around. *(20 sts)*

Rnd 3: [Sc in next sc, 2 sc in next sc] around. *(30 sts)*

Rnd 4: [Sc in each of next 4 sc, 2 sc in next sc] around. *(36 sts)*

Rnd 5: [Sc in each of next 5 sc, 2 sc in next sc] around. *(42 sts)*

Rnd 6: [Sc in each of next 2 sc, 2 sc in next sc] around. *(56 sts)*

Rnd 7: Sc in each sc around.

Rnd 8: [Sc in each of next 6 sc, 2 sc in next st] around. *(64 sts)*

Rnd 9: [Sc in each of next 7 sc, 2 sc in next st] around. *(72 sts)*

Rnd 10: [Sc in each of next 8 sc, 2 sc in next st] around. *(80 sts)*

Rnd 11: [Sc in each of next 9 sc, 2 sc in next st] around. *(88 sts)*

Rnds 12–26: Sc in each sc around. At end of last rnd, fasten off MC and attach CC.

Rnds 27–30: Now working with CC, sc in each sc around. At end of last rnd, fasten off CC and attach MC.

Rnds 31 & 32: Now working with MC, sc in each sc around.

Rnd 33: [Sc in next st, 2 sc in next st] around. *(132 sts)*

Rnds 34–42: Sc in each sc around. At end of last rnd, join with sl st in first st of last rnd. Fasten off.

Janie

Granddaughter Kodi currently is going through chemotherapy.

FLOWER

With CC, leaving a 12-inch length of yarn, ch 18, 2 dc in 3rd ch from hook, 3 dc in each of next 4 chs, 3 tr in each of next 4 chs, 2 dtr in each of next 6 chs, 5 dtr in last ch. **Do not fasten off**. Pull up long lp, and remove lp from hook. Beg at opposite end, roll based on natural tendency. When beg of Flower reaches 3rd tr of 4th 3-tr group, pin end of Flower to 3rd tr, then wrap remainder of Flower around outside of rolled Flower so that last dtr is placed behind pinned tr. Place lp on hook, shorten lp, join last dtr to pinned tr with sl st. Fasten off. Use 12-inch end to sew Flower as rolled, and to sew Flower to rows 27–30 of Hat as shown in photo.

CHILD'S FLOPPY HAT

SKILL LEVEL

EASY

FINISHED SIZE
One size fits most

FINISHED MEASUREMENT
Approx 18-inch circumference

MATERIALS
- Berroco Comfort medium (worsted) weight yarn (3½ oz/210 yds/100g per ball):
   1 ball each #9728 raspberry sorbet (*MC*) and #9793 boysenberry heather (*CC*)
- Size G/6/4mm hook or size needed to obtain gauge
- Stitch markers
- Safety pin

GAUGE
4 sc = 1 inch; 5 sc rnds = 1 inch

PATTERN NOTES
Hat is worked in continuous rounds.

Do not join or turn unless otherwise stated.

Place marker at end of each round to mark beginning of following round. Move marker as each round is completed.

INSTRUCTIONS
CHILD'S HAT
Rnd 1: With MC, ch 4, sl st in 4th ch from hook to form ring, ch 1, work 10 sc in ring, **do not join** (*see Pattern Notes*), **place marker** (*see Pattern Notes*). (*10 sc*)

Rnd 2: 2 sc in each sc around. (*20 sts*)

Rnd 3: [Sc in next sc, 2 sc in next sc] around. (*30 sts*)

Rnd 4: [Sc in each of next 4 sc, 2 sc in next sc] around. (*36 sts*)

Rnd 5: [Sc in each of next 5 sc, 2 sc in next sc] around. (*42 sts*)

Rnd 6: [Sc in each of next 2 sc, 2 sc in next sc] around. (*56 sts*)

Rnd 7: Sc in each sc around.

Rnd 8: [Sc in each of next 6 sc, 2 sc in next st] around. (*64 sts*)

Rnd 9: [Sc in each of next 7 sc, 2 sc in next st] around. (*72 sts*)

Rnds 10–18: Sc in each sc around. At end of last rnd, fasten off MC and attach CC.

Rnds 19–22: Now working with CC, sc in each sc around. At end of last rnd, fasten off CC and attach MC.

Rnds 23 & 24: Sc in each sc around.

Rnd 25: [Sc in next sc, 2 sc in next sc] around. (*108 sts*)

Rnds 26–32: Sc in each sc around. At end of last rnd, join with sl st in first st of last rnd. Fasten off.

FLOWER
With CC, leaving a 12-inch length of yarn, ch 18, 2 dc in 3rd ch from hook, 3 dc in each of next 4 chs, 3 tr in each of next 4 chs, 2 dtr in each of next 6 chs, 5 dtr in last ch. **Do not fasten off**. Pull up long lp and remove lp from hook. Beg at opposite end, roll, based on natural tendency. When beg of Flower reaches 3rd tr of 4th 3-tr group, pin end of Flower to 3rd tr, then wrap remainder of Flower around outside of rolled Flower so that last dtr is placed behind pinned tr. Place lp on hook, shorten lp, join last dtr to pinned tr with sl st. Fasten off. Use 12-inch end to sew Flower as rolled, and to sew Flower to rows 19–22 of Hat as shown in photo. ■

Barbra

Breast cancer survivor—13 years

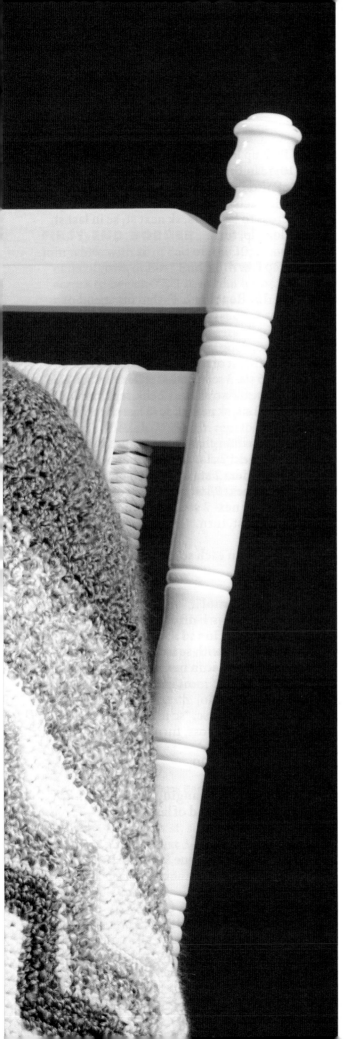

Ripple Wrap & Cap

DESIGNS BY **DOROTHY WARRELL**

SKILL LEVEL

◀■■☐▭
EASY

FINISHED SIZE

Cap: One size fits most

FINISHED MEASUREMENTS

Wrap: 23 x 50 inches

Cap: Approx 22-inch circumference

MATERIALS

- Lion Brand Homespun bulky (chunky) weight yarn (6 oz/ 185 yds/170g per skein):
    - 2 skeins #322 baroque
    - 1 skein #315 Tudor
- Lion Brand Vanna's Choice medium (worsted) weight yarn (3½ oz/ 170 yds/100g per skein):
    - 2 skeins #100 white
- Size H/8/5mm crochet hook or size needed to obtain gauge
- Stitch markers

GAUGE

6 sts = 2 inches; 3 rows or rnds = 1 inch

PATTERN NOTE

Join with slip stitch unless otherwise stated.

Rnd 5: With Tudor, rep rnd 2. Fasten off.

Rnd 6: Rep rnd 3.

Rnd 7: Join baroque with sc in first st, rep rnd 2.

Rnd 8: With baroque, rep rnd 2.

Rnd 9: Rep rnd 3.

Rnds 10 & 11: Rep rnds 4 and 5.

Rnd 12: Rep rnd 3.

Rnd 13: Rep rnd 7. Fasten off.

Rnd 14: Join white with sc in first st, ***sc dec** *(see Stitch Guide)* in next 2 sts, sc in each of next 4 sts, 3 sc in next st, sc in each of next 4 sts, sc dec in next 2 sts, sk next 2 sc, rep from * around, join in first st. *(65 sc)*

Rnd 15: Ch 1, *sc dec in next 2 sts, sc in each of next 3 sts, 3 sc in next st, sc in each of next 3 sts, sc dec in next 2 sts, sk next 2 sts, rep from * around, join in first st. *(55 sc)*

Rnd 16: Ch 1, *sc dec in next 2 sts, sc in each of next 2 sts, 3 sc in next st, sc in each of next 2 sts, sc dec in next 2 sts, sk next 2 sts, rep from * around, join in first st. *(45 sc)*

Rnd 17: Ch 1, *sc dec in next 2 sts, sc in next st, 3 sc in next st, sc in next st, sc dec in next 2 sts, sk next 2 sts, rep from * around, join in first st. Fasten off. *(35 sc)*

Rnd 18: Join baroque with sc in first st, sc in each rem st around, join in first st. Fasten off.

Rnd 19: Join white with sc in first st, [sc in each of next 3 sts, sc dec in next 2 sts] 7 times. *(28 sc)*

Rnd 20: [Sc in each of next 2 sts, sc dec in next 2 sts] 7 times. *(21 sc)*

Rnd 21: [Sc in next sc, sc dec in next 2 sts] 7 times. Leaving a 12-inch end for sewing, fasten off.

ASSEMBLY

Weave long end through sts from rnd 21. Gather sts tightly, and fasten off.

BRIM

Rnd 1: Join white in rem lp of first ch of foundation ch, sc in each of next 2 chs, *hdc in each of next 2 chs, dc in each of next 2 chs, tr in each of next 2 chs, dc in each of next 2 chs, hdc in each of next 2 chs, sc in each of next 3 chs, rep from * around to last st, sc in last st. Do not join or turn. Mark end of each rnd.

Rnd 2: Ch 1, sc in each st around. *(75 sc)*

Rnd 3: 2 sc in first st, *sc in each of next 13 sts, 2 sc in next st, rep from * 5 times, sc in each rem st around. *(81 sc)*

Rnd 4: 2 sc in first st, *sc in each of next 14 sts, 2 sc in next st, rep from * 5 times, sc in each rem st around. *(87 sc)*

Rnd 5: 2 sc in first st, *sc in each of next 15 sts, 2 sc in next st, rep from * 5 times, sc in each rem st around. *(93 sc)*

Rnd 6: 2 sc in first st, *sc in each of next 16 sts, 2 sc in next st, rep from * 5 times, sc in each rem st around. *(99 sc)*

Rnds 7–12: Sc in each sc around. *(99 sc)*

Rnd 13: Sc dec in first 2 sts, *sc in each of next 16 sts, sc dec in next 2 sts, rep from * 5 times, sc in each rem st around.

Rnd 14: Sc dec in first 2 sts, *sc in each of next 15 sts, sc dec in next 2 sts, rep from * 5 times, sc in each rem st around.

Rnd 15: Sc dec in first 2 sts, *sc in each of next 14 sts, sc dec in next 2 sts, rep from * 5 times, sc in each rem st around.

Rnd 16: Sc dec in first 2 sts, *sc in each of next 13 sts, sc dec in next 2 sts, rep from * 5 times, sc in each rem st around. *(75 sc)*

Rnd 17: Sc in each sc around. Leaving 12-inch end, fasten off. Fold half of Brim to inside of Cap. Using 12-inch length, loosely sew last rnd of Brim to top of first rnd of Brim. If desired, place over a mold and steam lightly to shape. ∎

Miss Chloe Cap

DESIGN BY **BEVERLY MATHESON**

SKILL LEVEL

■■■□
INTERMEDIATE

FINISHED SIZE
One size fits most

FINISHED MEASUREMENT
Approx 19-inch circumference

MATERIALS
- Lion Brand Vanna's Choice medium (worsted) weight yarn (3 oz/ 145 yds/85g per ball):
    1 ball each #301 rose mist *(MC)*, #303 purple mist *(CC)*
- Size H/8/5mm crochet hook or size needed to obtain gauge

GAUGE
4 sts = 1 inch; 2 dc rnds = 1 inch; 4 sc rnds = 1 inch

PATTERN NOTES
Join rounds with slip stitch unless otherwise stated.

Chain-3 at beginning of round counts as first double crochet unless otherwise stated.

SPECIAL STITCHES
V-stitch (V-st): (Dc, ch 2, dc) in indicated sp.

Single crochet V-stitch (sc V-st): (2 sc, ch 1, 2 sc) in indicated sp.

INSTRUCTIONS
CAP
Rnd 1 (RS): With MC, ch 4, **join** *(see Pattern Notes)* in 4th ch from hook to form ring, **ch 3** *(see Pattern Notes)*, 2 dc in ring, ch 1, *3 dc in ring, ch 1, rep from * 3 times, join in top of beg ch-3. *(15 dc, 5 ch-1 sps)*

Rnd 2: Ch 3, dc in each of next 2 dc, **V-st** *(see Special Stitches)* in next ch-1 sp, *dc in each of next 3 dc, V-st in next ch-1 sp, rep from * around, join in top of beg ch-3. *(15 dc, 5 V-sts)*

Rnd 3: Ch 3, dc in each of next 3 dc, *V-st in next ch-2 sp**, dc in each of next 5 dc, rep from * around, ending last rep at **, dc in next dc, join in top of beg ch-3. *(25 dc, 5 V-sts)*

Rnd 4: Ch 3, dc in each of next 4 dc, *V-st in next ch-2 sp**, dc in each of next 7 dc, rep from * around, ending last rep at **, dc in each of next 2 dc, join in top of beg ch-3. *(35 dc, 5 V-sts)*

Rnd 5: Ch 1, sc in same st as beg ch-1, sc in each of next 5 dc, *sc **V-st** *(see Special Stitches)* in next ch-2 sp**, sc in each of next 9 dc, rep from * around, ending last rep at **, sc in each of next 3 dc, join with CC in first sc. *(45 sc, 5 V-sts)*

Rnd 6: With CC, ch 1, sc in same st as beg ch-1, *sc in each sc across to next ch-1 sp, 2 sc in next ch-1 sp, rep from * 4 times, sc in each sc across to first sc, join in first sc. *(75 sc)*

Rnd 7: Ch 1, sc in same sc as beg ch-1, sc in each rem sc around, join in first sc.

Rnd 8: Ch 1, sc in same sc as beg ch-1, sc in each rem sc around, join with MC in first sc.

Rnds 9 & 10: With MC, ch 1, sc in same sc as beg ch-1, sc in each rem sc around, join in first sc.

Rnd 11: Ch 1, sc in same sc as beg ch-1, sc in each of next 22 sc, **sc dec** *(see Stitch Guide)* in next 2 sc, [sc in each of next 23 sc, sc dec in next 2 sc] twice, join with CC in first sc. *(72 sc)*

Rnd 12: With CC, ch 1, sc in same sc as beg ch-1, *ch 5, sc in 2nd ch from hook, hdc in next ch, dc in next ch, tr in next ch, sk next 3 sc**, sc in next sc, rep from * around, ending last rep at **, join with MC in first sc.

Rnd 13: With MC, ch 5, *sc in tip of next ch-5, sc in next sc, hdc in next hdc, dc in next dc, tr in next tr, rep from * around, sk beg ch-5, join with CC in first sc.

Rnd 14: With CC, sl st in next sc, ch 1, sc in same sc as beg ch-1, sc in each of next 3 sc, *sk next sc, sc in each of next 4 sc, rep from * around, join with MC in first sc. *(72 sc)*

Rnd 15: With MC, ch 1, sc in same sc as beg ch-1, *ch 5, sc in 2nd ch from hook, hdc in next ch, dc in next ch, tr in next ch, sk next 3 sc**, sc in

next sc, rep from * around, ending last rep at **, join with CC in first sc.

Rnd 16: With CC, ch 5, *sc in tip of next ch-5, sc in next sc, hdc in next hdc, dc in next dc, tr in next tr, rep from * around, sk beg ch-5, join with MC in first sc.

Rnd 17: With MC, sl st in next sc, ch 1, sc in same sc as beg ch-1, sc in each of next 3 sts, *sk next sc, sc in each of next 4 sts, rep from * around, join in first sc. *(72 sc)*

Rnd 18: Ch 1, sc in same sc as beg ch-1, sc in each rem sc around, join in first sc.

Rnd 19: Ch 1, sc in same sc as beg ch-1, sc in each rem sc around, join with CC in first sc.

Rnds 20 & 21: With CC, rep rnd 18.

Rnd 22: Ch 1, sc in same sc as beg ch-1, sc in each rem sc around, join with MC in first sc.

Rnd 23: With MC, ch 1, sc in same sc as beg ch-1, sc in each rem sc around, join in first sc. Fasten off.

Weave in ends. ∎

Becky

Crochet designer and breast cancer survivor—9 years

I was diagnosed with breast cancer in 2001 at the age of 57. It was quite a surprise since there was no history of breast cancer in my family. I underwent two surgeries for a lumpectomy, six months of chemo and six weeks of radiation. I am completely cancer free and healthy. Since we live close to Washington, D.C., I try to walk in the national Susan G. Komen Race for the Cure every June to celebrate my life and those of other survivors as well as remember all those who weren't as fortunate. When I was finishing my treatment, my son walked in the Komen Race for the Cure in 2002. He wore a placard with my name on it to celebrate my survival. For Christmas that year, he gave me that placard and his race bib, one of the best presents I ever received.

Ribbed Cap

DESIGN BY **BECKY STEVENS**

SKILL LEVEL

EASY

FINISHED SIZE
One size fits most

FINISHED MEASUREMENTS
Approx 20-inch circumference

MATERIALS
- Deborah Norville Serenity Chunky bulky (chunky) weight yarn (3½ oz/ 109 yds/100g per ball):
    2 balls #DN700-21 pristine
- Size K/10½/6.5mm crochet hook or size needed to obtain gauge

GAUGE
3 sc = 1 inch; 3 sc rows = 1 inch; 5 dc (3 fpdc and 2 bpdc **or** 3 bpdc and 2 fpdc) = 2 inches; 5 rnds = 2 inches

PATTERN NOTES
Join with slip stitch unless otherwise stated.

Chain-2 at beginning of round counts as first double crochet unless otherwise stated.

SPECIAL STITCH
Front post double crochet decrease (fpdc dec):
    Keeping last lp of each fpdc on hook, fpdc around indicated sts, yo, draw lp through all lps on hook.

INSTRUCTIONS
RIBBING
Row 1: Ch 7, sc in 2nd ch from hook and each rem ch across, turn. *(6 sc)*

*Note: From this point on, ribbing rows are worked in **back lps** (see Stitch Guide) unless otherwise stated.*

Rows 2–50: Ch 1, sc in **back lp** *(see Note)* of each st across, turn.

Row 51 (joining row): Working in back lps of previous row and in starting ch on opposite side of row 1, ch 1, sl st in each st across, turn. Do not fasten off.

BODY
Rnd 1: Now working in rnds around top of Ribbing, sc in end of each row around, **join** *(see Pattern Notes)* in first sc. *(50 sc)*

Rnd 2: Ch 2 *(see Pattern Notes)*, dc in each st around, join in top of beg ch-2. *(50 sts)*

Rnd 3: Ch 2, **fpdc** *(see Stitch Guide)* around next ch-2, *bpdc *(see Stitch Guide)* around next dc, *fpdc around next dc, bpdc around next dc on row below, rep from * around, join in top of beg ch-2.

Rnds 4–10: Ch 2, *fpdc around next fpdc, bpdc around next bpdc, rep from * around, join in top of beg ch-2.

Rnd 11: Ch 2, *fpdc around next fpdc, sk next bpdc, rep from * around, join in top of beg ch-2.

Rnd 12: Ch 2, fpdc around each fpdc around, join in top of beg ch-2.

Rnd 13: Ch 2, ***fpdc dec** *(see Special Stitch)* around next 2 fpdc, rep from * around to last fpdc, fpdc around last fpdc, join in top of beg ch-2.

Rnd 14: Ch 2, *fpdc dec around next 2 fpdc dec, rep from * around to last fpdc dec, fpdc around last fpdc dec, join in top of beg ch-2. Leaving 12-inch length, fasten off.

FINISHING
Weave 12-inch length twice through last rnd of Hat, pull tight. Fasten off and weave in ends. ∎

Nancy
Skin cancer survivor—11 years

Simple Shells Shawl

DESIGN BY **DARLA FANTON**

SKILL LEVEL

INTERMEDIATE

FINISHED MEASUREMENTS

Approx 50 inches across top x 33 inches long

MATERIALS

- NaturallyCaron.com Spa light (light worsted) weight yarn (3 oz/ 251 yds/85g per ball): 3 balls #0004 green sheen
- Size L/11/8mm crochet hook or size needed to obtain gauge

GAUGE

1 shell = 1½ inches wide; 3 rows = 3 inches

SPECIAL STITCHES

Beginning shell (beg shell): Ch 3 *(counts as first dc)*, 4 dc in same st as beg ch-3.

Shell: 5 dc in indicated st or sp.

Picot: Ch 3, sl st in 3rd ch from hook.

INSTRUCTIONS

SHAWL

Row 1: Ch 2, **shell** *(see Special Stitches)* in 2nd ch from hook, turn. *(1 shell)*

Row 2: **Beg shell** *(see Special Stitches)* in first st, [sk next st, shell in next st] twice, turn. *(3 shells)*

Row 3: Beg shell in first st, sk next st, hdc in next st, sk next st, shell in next st, [sk next 2 sts, shell in next st] twice, sk next st, hdc in next st, sk next st, shell in last st, turn. *(5 shells, 2 hdc)*

Row 4: Beg shell in first st, sk next st, hdc in next st, sk next 2 sts, shell in next st, sk next 2 sts, hdc in next, sk next 2 sts, shell in next st, [sk next st, shell in next st] twice, sk next 2 sts, hdc in next st, sk next 2 sts, shell in next st, sk next 2 sts, hdc in next st, sk next st, shell in last st, turn. *(7 shells, 4 hdc)*

Row 5: Beg shell in first st, sk next st, [hdc in next st, sk next 2 sts, shell in next st, sk next 2 sts] across to shell before center shell, hdc in next st, sk next 2 sts, shell in next st, [sk next st, shell in next st] twice, [sk next 2 sts, hdc in next st, sk next 2 sts, shell in next st] across to last shell, sk next 2 sts, hdc in next st, sk next st, shell in last st, turn. *(9 shells, 6 hdc)*

Rows 6–25: Rep row 5. **Do not turn** at end of last row. *(49 shells, 46 hdc at end of last row)*

Rnd 26: Now working in rnds, beg shell in first st, sk next st, [hdc in next st, sk next 2 sts, shell in next st, sk next 2 sts] across to shell before center shell, hdc in next st, sk next 2 sts, shell in next st, [sk next st, shell in next st] twice, [sk next 2 sts, hdc in next st, sk next 2 sts, shell in next st] across to last shell, sk next 2 sts, hdc in next st, sk next st, 2 shells in last st, now working in ends of rows, [hdc in end of next row, shell in end of next row] across to end of last 2 rows, hdc in end of next row, shell in same st as beg shell, do not turn.

Row 27: Now working in rows, sc in top of beg ch-3 of next beg shell, sc in next st, [(sc, **picot**— *see Special Stitches*, sc) in next st, sc in each of next 2 sts] 47 times, sc in each of next 2 sts, (sc, picot, sc) in next st, sc in each of next 4 sts, [(sc, picot, sc) in next st, sc in each of next 2 sts] 47 times, sl st in next st. Fasten off. *(95 picots)*

Weave in ends. ■

Easy Beanie

DESIGN BY **MARGARET HUBERT**

SKILL LEVEL

EASY

FINISHED SIZE
One size fits most

FINISHED MEASUREMENT
Approx 22-inch circumference

MATERIALS
- Plymouth Yarn Fantasy Naturale medium (worsted) weight yarn (3½ oz/140 yds/100g per hank): 1 hank each #7382 brown (*MC*) and #8990 black (*CC*)
- Sizes I/9/5.5mm and J/10/6mm crochet hooks or size needed to obtain gauge

GAUGE
Size J hook: 12 sc = 4 inches

PATTERN NOTES
Change colors every 2 rows, but do not fasten off. Carry up sides.

Work rows in **back loops** (*see Stitch Guide*) unless otherwise stated.

INSTRUCTIONS
BEANIE
Foundation row: With CC, ch 26, sc in 2nd ch from hook and in each rem ch across, **changing color** (*see Stitch Guide*) to MC in last st, **do not fasten off CC** (*see Pattern Notes*), turn. (*25 sc*)

Row 1 (RS): Working in **back lps** (*see Pattern Notes*), with MC, ch 1, sk first sc, sc in each of next 4 sc, hdc in each of next 20 sc, turn.

Row 2: Ch 2, sk first st, hdc in each of next 19 hdc, sc in each of next 4 sc, changing color to CC, sc in beg ch-1 sp, turn.

Row 3: With CC, ch 1, sk first sc, sc in each st across row, sc in beg ch-2 sp, turn.

Row 4: Ch 1, sk first sc, sc in each st across row, changing color to MC, sc in beg ch-2 sp, turn.

Row 5: With MC, ch 2, sk first sc, sc in each of next 4 sc, hdc in each of next 19 sc, hdc in beg ch-1 sp, turn.

Row 6: Ch 2, sk first st, hdc in each of next 19 hdc, sc in each of next 4 sc, changing color to CC, sc in beg ch-1 sp, turn.

Next rows: Rep rows 3–6 until Beanie has 13 brown ribs.

Last row: Rep row 3.

EDGING
Rnd 1: Now working in rnds around bottom edge of Beanie, with size I hook and CC, work *evenly sp 3 sc in edge of each CC rib and 2 sc in edge of each MC rib, rep from * around, join with sl st in first sc. (*65 sc*)

Rnd 2: Ch 1, sc in each sc around. Fasten off.

FINISHING
Leaving a 36-inch length of yarn for sewing, sew foundation row to last row of Beanie, gather ends of rows at top of Beanie with same yarn, secure tightly. Fasten off. ■

Margaret

Crochet designer and cancer survivor

Miss Maisy's Slouch Cap

DESIGN BY **BEVERLY MATHESON**

FINISHED SIZE
Approx 24-inch circumference

MATERIALS
- I Love This Yarn medium (worsted) weight yarn (7 oz/355 yds/194g per skein):
  - 1 skein #320 sea blue
- Size F/5/3.75mm crochet hook or size needed to obtain gauge
- 1-inch button (larger if desired) (optional)

GAUGE
Rnds 1 and 2 = 4 inches in diameter; 4 hdc = 1 inch; 3 hdc rnds = 1 inch

PATTERN NOTES
Join with slip stitch unless otherwise stated.

Chain-4 counts as first treble crochet unless otherwise stated.

SPECIAL STITCHES
Beginning popcorn (beg pc): Ch 4 (*see Pattern Notes*), 3 tr in indicated st, drop last lp from hook, insert hook into top of beg ch-3, pick up dropped lp and draw lp through.

Popcorn (pc): 4 tr in the indicated st, drop last lp from hook, insert hook into first tr, pick up dropped lp and draw lp through.

Shell: Ch 3, 2 dc in indicated st or sp.

INSTRUCTIONS
CAP
Rnd 1: Ch 7, **join** (*see Pattern Notes*) in 7th ch from hook to form ring, **beg pc** (*see Special Stitches*) in ring, ch 3, [**pc** (*see Special Stitches*) in ring, ch 3] 5 times, join in top of beg pc. (*6 pc*)

Rnd 2: Ch 4 (*see Pattern Notes*), 2 tr into same st as beg ch-3, *5 tr in next ch-3 sp**, 3 tr in top of next pc, rep from * around, ending last rep at **, join in top of beg ch-4. (*48 tr*)

Rnd 3: Beg pc in same st as join, ch 3, *sk next tr, pc in next tr, ch 3, rep from * around, join in top of first pc. (*24 pc*)

Rnd 4: Ch 1, sc in same pc as beg ch-1, 3 sc in next ch-3 sp, [sc in next pc, 3 sc in next ch-3 sp] around, join in first sc. (*96 sc*)

Rnd 5: Ch 4, sk same st as join, tr in each rem st around, join in top of beg ch-4. (*96 tr*)

Rnd 6: Ch 1, sc in each st around, join in first st. (*96 sc*)

Rnds 7–14: Hdc in each st around, join in first st. (*96 hdc*)

Rnd 15: Shell (*see Special Stitches*) in same st as join, sk next 2 sts, sc in next st**, shell in same st as sc, rep from * around ending last rep at **, join in ch-3 sp of first shell.

Rnd 16: Shell in same ch-3 sp as join, *sk next 3 sts, sc in next ch-3 sp, shell in same ch-3 sp as sc, rep from * around, join in ch-3 sp of first shell.

Rnd 17: Ch 3, *sc in top of next ch-3, sk next st, hdc in next st*, rep * around, join in first sc. *(64 sts)*

Rnds 18–21: Ch 1, hdc in each st around, join in first hdc. *(64 hc)*

FLOWER

Rnd 1: Ch 7, join in 7th ch from hook to form ring, **beg pc** *(see Special Stitches)* in ring, ch 3, [**pc** *(see Special Stitches)* in ring, ch 3] 5 times, join in top of beg pc. *(6 pc)*

Rnd 2: Ch 3, sc in same st as join, *ch 3, sc in next ch-3 sp, [ch 3, sc in same ch-3 sp] twice, ch 3**, sc in top of next pc, rep from * around, ending last rep at **, join in top of beg ch-3. Fasten off.

ASSEMBLY

Place Flower on Cap where desired, and sew to Cap. Sew button to center of Flower. ■

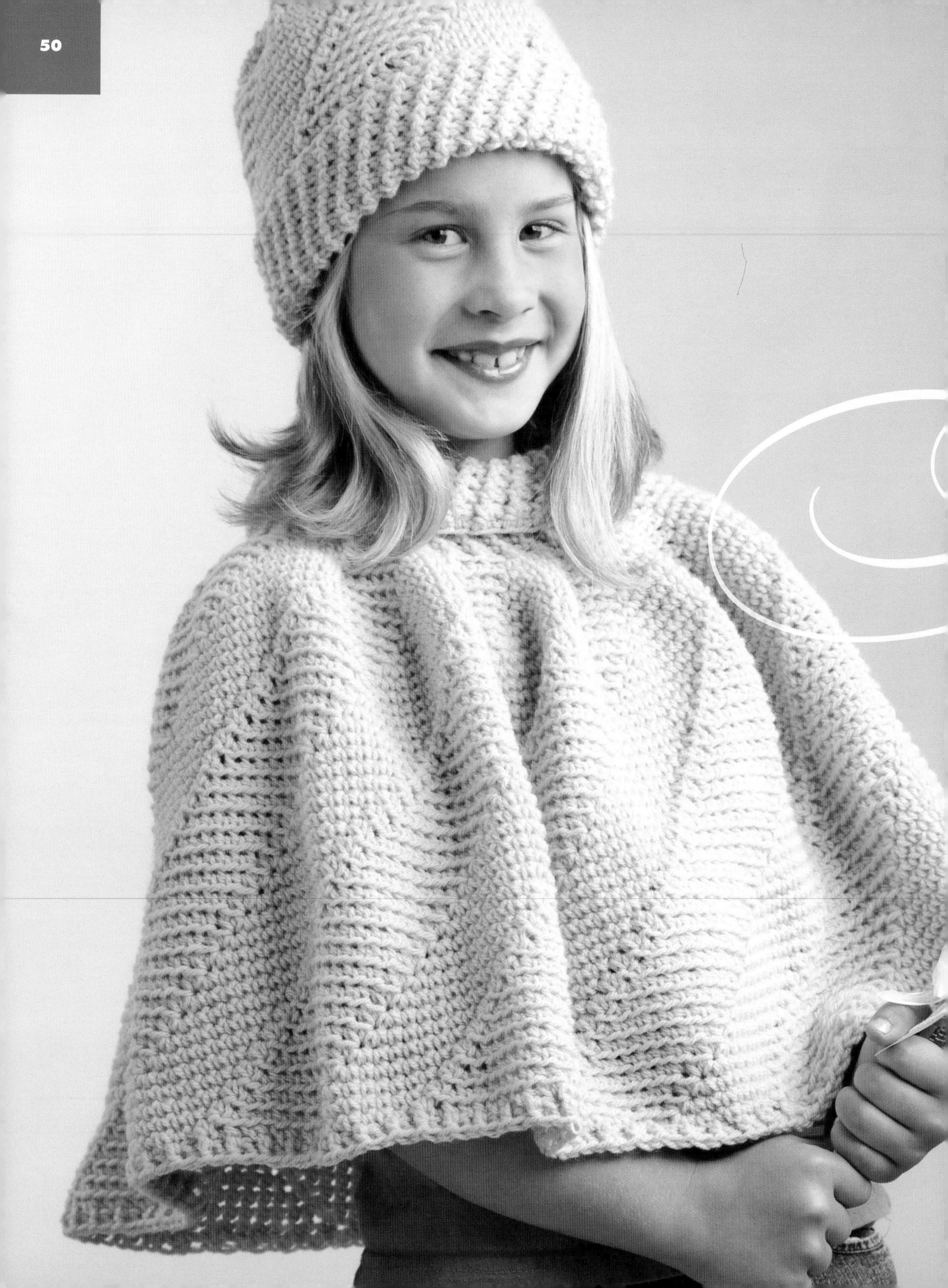

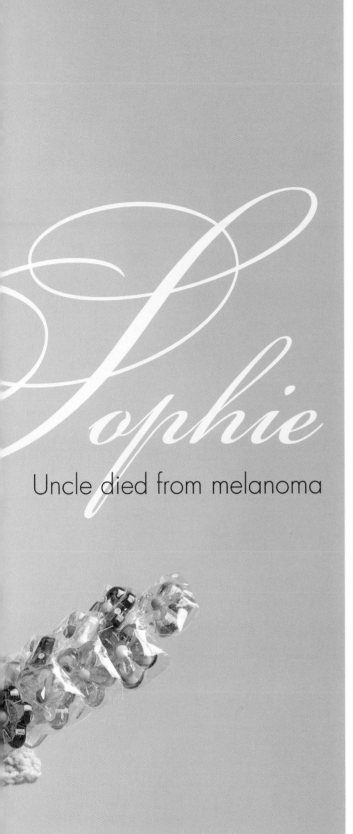

Sophie

Uncle died from melanoma

Knit-Look
Cap &
Poncho

DESIGNS BY **BENDY CARTER**

SKILL LEVEL

EASY

FINISHED SIZES
Cap: Instructions given fit small/medium; changes for medium/large are in [ ].

Poncho: Instructions given fit child's size 2–4; changes for sizes 6–8 and 10–12 are in [ ].

FINISHED MEASUREMENTS
Cap: 10 [11½] inches long, with Ribbing unfolded

Poncho: 15¼ [17¾, 21¼] inches long, with Ribbing unfolded

MATERIALS
- Red Heart Designer Sport light (light worsted) weight yarn (3 oz/ 279 yds/85g per ball): 4 [5, 6] balls #3620 celadon
- Size H/8/5mm crochet hook or size needed to obtain gauge

GAUGE
8 sts = 2 inches; 8 rnds = 2 inches

Take time to check gauge.

PATTERN NOTES
Cap is worked in continuous rounds.

Do not join or turn unless otherwise stated.

SPECIAL STITCHES

Front post single crochet (fpsc):
Insert hook from front to back to front around post of indicated st on previous row, draw lp through, complete as sc.

Back post single crochet (bpsc):
Insert hook from back to front to back around post of indicated st on previous row, draw lp through, complete as sc.

INSTRUCTIONS

CAP
TOP
Rnd 1 (RS): Ch 2, 8 sc in 2nd ch from hook, **do not join** (*see Pattern Notes*). (*8 sts*)

Rnd 2: Working in continuous rnds (*see Pattern Notes*), [2 sc in next st, 2 sc in **back lp** (*see Stitch Guide*) of next st] 4 times. (*16 sts*)

Rnd 3: [2 sc in next st, sc in next st, 2 sc in back lp of next st, sc in back lp of next st] 4 times. (*24 sts*)

Rnd 4: [2 sc in next st, sc in each of next 2 sts, 2 sc in back lp of next st, sc in back lp of each of next 2 sts] 4 times. (*32 sts*)

Rnd 5: [2 sc in next st, sc in each of next 3 sts, 2 sc in back lp of next st, sc in back lp of each of next 3 sts] 4 times. (*40 sts*)

Rnd 6: [2 sc in next st, sc in each of next 4 sts, 2 sc in back lp of next st, sc in back lp of each of next 4 sts] 4 times. (*48 sts*)

Rnd 7: [2 sc in next st, sc in each of next 5 sts, 2 sc in back lp of next st, sc in back lp of each of next 5 sts] 4 times. (*56 sts*)

Rnd 8: [2 sc in next st, sc in each of next 6 sts, 2 sc in back lp of next st, sc in back lp of each of next 6 sts] 4 times. (*64 sts*)

Rnd 9: [2 sc in next st, sc in each of next 7 sts, 2 sc in back lp of next st, sc in back lp of each of next 7 sts] 4 times. (*72 sts*)

SIZE MEDIUM/LARGE ONLY
Rnd [10]: [2 sc in next st, sc in each of next [8] sts, 2 sc in back lp of next st, sc in back lp of each of next [8] sts] 4 times. (*[80] sts*)

BOTH SIZES

Rnd 11 [12]: [2 sc in next st, sc in each of next 6 [7] sts, **sc dec** *(see Stitch Guide)* in next 2 sts, 2 sc in back lp of next st, sc in back lp of each of next 6 [7] sts, sc dec in back lp of next 2 sts] 4 times. *(72 [80] sts)*

Next rnds: Rep rnd 11 until Cap measures 6 [6½] inches from beg of Top.

RIBBING

Rnd 1: [**Fpsc** *(see Special Stitches)* around next st, **bpsc** *(see Special Stitches)* around next st] around.

Next rnds: Rep rnd 1 until Ribbing measures 4 [5] inches from beg. At end of last rnd, join with sl st in first st of last rnd. Fasten off.

Fold Ribbing in half.

BUTTON

Ch 4, sl st in **back bar of beg ch** *(see illustration)* to form ring, sl st in back bar of each ch around, join with sl st in beg sl st. Fasten off, leaving long tail for sewing. Sew Button to Top of Cap.

Back Bar of Chain

PONCHO
NECK RIBBING

Rnd 1: Ch 72 [72, 80], being careful not to twist ch, sc in **back bar of beg ch** *(see illustration)* to form ring, sc in back bar of each ch around, **do not join** *(see Pattern Notes)*. *(72 [72, 80] sts)*

Rnd 2: [**Fpsc** *(see Special Stitches)* around next st, **bpsc** *(see Special Stitches)* around next st] around.

Next rnds: Rep rnd 2 until Neck Ribbing measures 4 [4, 5] inches from beg. **Do not fasten off** at end of last rnd. *(72 [72, 80] sts at end of last rnd)*

BODY
SIZE 2-4 ONLY

Rnd 1: Sc in each st around. *(72 sts)*

SIZE 6-8 ONLY

Rnd [1]: *Sc in each of next [5] sts, 2 sc in next st, rep from * around. *([84] sts)*

SIZE 10-12 ONLY

Rnd [1]: Sc in each of next [19] sts, 2 sc in next st, rep from * around *([84] sts)*

ALL SIZES

Rnd 2: [2 sc in next st, sc in each of next 2 sts, 2 sc in **back lp** *(see Stitch Guide)* of next st, sc in back lp of each of next 2 sts] around. *(96 [112, 112] sts)*

Rnd 3: [2 sc in next st, sc in each of next 3 sts, 2 sc in back lp of next st, sc in back lp of each of next 3 sts] around. *(120 [140, 140] sts)*

Rnd 4: [2 sc in next st, sc in each of next 4 sts, 2 sc in back lp of next st, sc in back lp of each of next 4 sts] around. *(144 [168, 168] sts)*

Rnd 5: [2 sc in next st, sc in each of next 5 sts, 2 sc in back lp of next st, sc in back lp of each of next 5 sts] around. *(168 [196, 196] sts)*

Rnd 6: [2 sc in next st, sc in each of next 6 sts, 2 sc in back lp of next st, sc in back lp of each of next 6 sts] around. *(192 [224, 224] sts)*

Rnd 7: [2 sc in next st, sc in each of next 7 sts, 2 sc in back lp of next st, sc in back lp of each of next 7 sts] around. *(216 [252, 252] sts)*

SIZE 10-12 ONLY

Rnd [8]: [2 sc in next st, sc in each of next [8] sts, 2 sc in back lp of next st, sc in back lp of each of next [8] sts] around. *([280] sts)*

ALL SIZES

Rnd 8 [8, 9]: [2 sc in next st, sc in each of next 6 [6, 7] sts, **sc dec** *(see Stitch Guide)* in next 2 sts, 2 sc in back lp of next st, sc in back lp of each of next 6 [6, 7] sts, sc dec in back lps of next 2 sts] around. *(216 [252, 280] sts)*

Next rnds: Rep rnd 9 until Poncho measures 11 [13½, 16] inches from beg of Body.

Last rnd: [Fpsc around next st, bpsc around next st] around, join with sl st in first st of last rnd. Fasten off. ∎

Leola

Daughter-in-law Judy is a 20-year breast cancer survivor

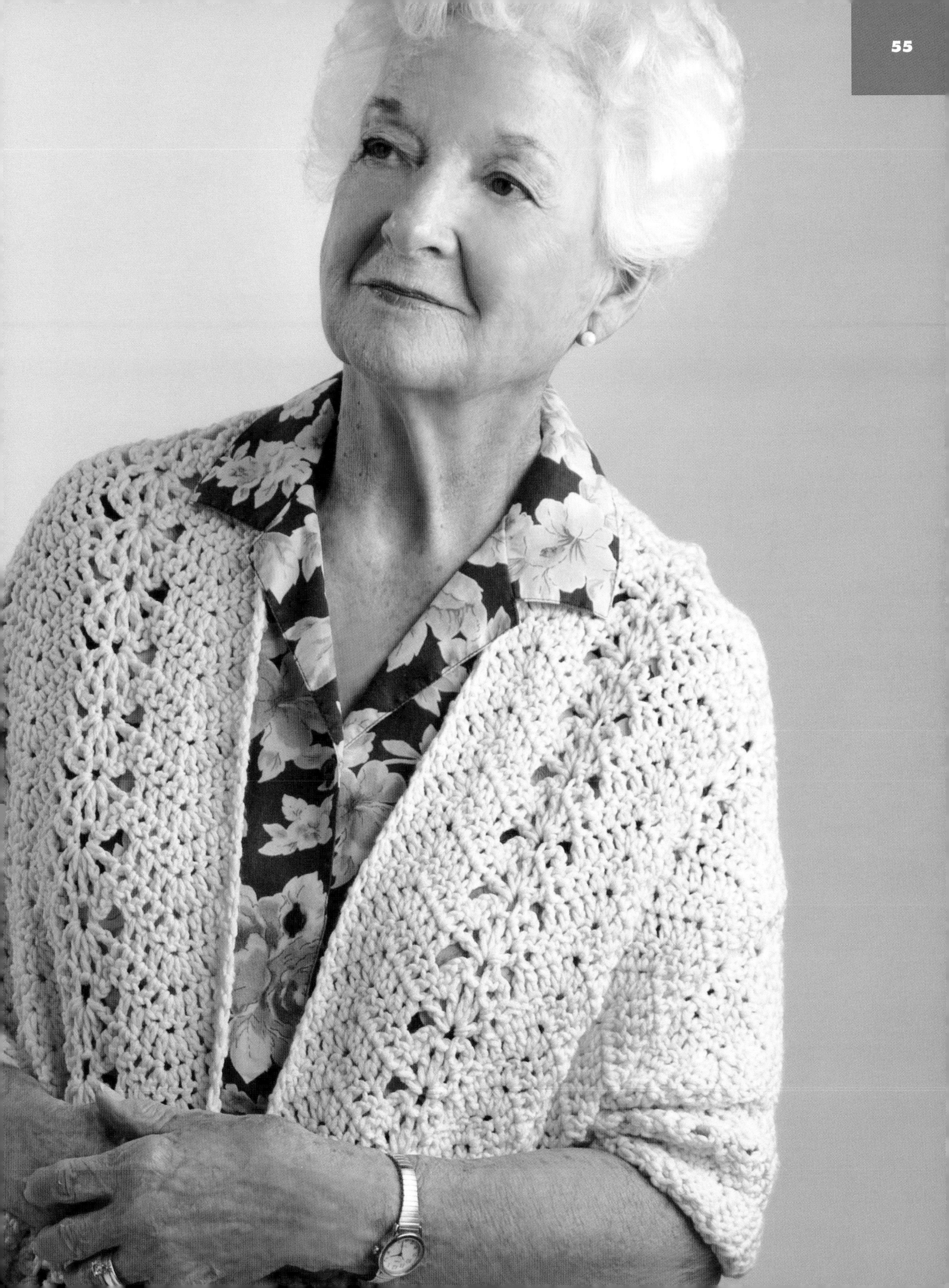

Sunshine Shawl

DESIGN BY **BECKY STEVENS**

SKILL LEVEL

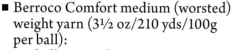

EASY

FINISHED MEASUREMENTS
20 x 60 inches

MATERIALS
- Berroco Comfort medium (worsted) weight yarn (3½ oz/210 yds/100g per ball):
    5 balls #9712 buttercup
- Size H/8/5mm crochet hook or size needed to obtain gauge

GAUGE
3 sts = 1 inch; 2 rows = 1 inch

PATTERN NOTES
Shawl is worked in a multiple of 14 plus 12. To make shawl wider, add rows in that increment.

Chain-2 at beginning of row counts as first double crochet unless otherwise stated.

INSTRUCTIONS
SHAWL
Row 1: Ch 68 loosely, sc in 2nd ch and each rem ch across, turn. (*67 sts*)

Row 2: Ch 2 (*see Pattern Notes*), sk same st as beg ch-2, sk next st, dc in each of next 3 sts, 3 dc in next st, dc in each of next 3 sts, *sk next 3 sts, ({dc, ch 1} 4 times, dc) in next st, sk next 3 sts, dc in each of next 3 sts, 3 dc in next st, dc in each of next 3 sts, rep from * 3 more times, sk next st, dc in last st, turn.

Row 3: Ch 2, sk same st as beg ch-2 and next st, dc in each of next 3 sts, 3 dc in next st, dc in each of next 3 sts, *sk next 2 dc, [(sc, ch 3) in next ch-1 sp] 3 times, sc in next ch-1 sp, sk next 2 dc, dc in each of next 3 dc, 3 dc in next st, dc in each of next 3 sts, rep from * 3 more times, sk last dc and work dc in top of beg ch-2, turn.

Row 4: Ch 2, sk same st as beg ch-2, sk next st, dc in each of next 3 sts, 3 dc in next st, dc in each of next 3 sts, *sk next dc, sc, ch-3 sp and sc, ({dc, ch 1} 4 times, dc) in center ch-3 sp, sk next sc, ch-3 sp, sc and dc, dc in each of next 3 dc, 3 dc in next st, dc in each of next 3 sts, rep from * across to last 2 dc, sk next dc, dc in top of beg ch-2.

Rows 5–104: [Rep rows 3 and 4 alternately] 52 times or until Shawl reaches desired length, ending with row 4, turn.

Row 105: Ch 1, sc in each st and ch-1 sp across. Fasten off and weave in ends. ∎

Tatyana

My friend had breast cancer and went through chemotherapy. She lost all her hair. I made this cap for her to wish her a quick recovery and to let her know I cared. She loved the cap and is doing much better now.

Spiral Cap

DESIGN BY **TATYANA MIRER**

SKILL LEVEL

EASY

FINISHED SIZE

Cap: One size fits most

FINISHED MEASUREMENTS

Cap: Approx 21¼-inch circumference

Lap robe: 26½ x 37 inches

MATERIALS

- Caron Simply Soft medium (worsted) weight yarn (6 oz/315 yds/170g per skein):
  3 skeins #9742 grey heather
  1 skein each #9727 black and #9701 white
- Size I/9/5.5mm crochet hook or size needed to obtain gauge

GAUGE

8 sc = 2 inches; 4 sc rows = 1 inch

PATTERN NOTES

In rows that use 2 colors, carry color not in use behind.

Work over color not in use until needed.

INSTRUCTIONS

CAP

Row 1: With grey heather, ch 27, sc in 2nd ch from hook and in each rem sc across, turn. *(26 sc)*

Rows 2–4: Ch 1, sc in each sc across, turn.

Row 5: Ch 1, sc in each sc across, **changing colors** *(see Stitch Guide)* to black in last sc, turn. Fasten off grey heather.

Row 6: With black, ch 1, sc in each sc across, changing colors to white in last sc, turn. **Do not fasten off** black.

Rows 7 & 8: With white, ch 1, sc in each sc across, turn.

Rows 9 & 10: **Carry black behind** *(see Pattern Notes)*, ch 1, with white, **working over black** *(see*

Pattern Notes), sc in each of first 2 sts, *pick up black, carry white behind, with black, working over white, sc in each of next 2 sts, pick up white, carry black behind, sc in each of next 2 sts, rep from * across, turn. Drop white at end of last row.

Rows 11 & 12: With black, ch 1, sc in each sc across, turn.

Rows 13 & 14: Rep rows 9 and 10. Drop black at end of last row.

Rows 15 & 16: With white, ch 1, sc in each sc across, turn.

Row 17: Pick up black, with black, ch 1, sc in each sc across, draw up long lp, drop lp from hook, do not turn. Fasten off black.

Row 18: Join grey heather with sc in first sc on last row, sc in each sc across to last sc, sc in last sc and in rem lp from last row, tighten lp.

Rows 19–22: With grey heather, rep rows 2–5.

Rows 23–35: Rep rows 6–18.

Rows 36–85: [Rep rows 19–35 consecutively] 3 times, ending last rep with row 34. Fasten off and weave in all ends.

BRIM

Row 1 (WS): With WS facing, working in ends of Cap rows and over any carried yarn, join grey heather with sc in end of row 85 of Cap, sc in end of each row across, turn.

Rows 2–14: Ch 1, sc in each sc across, turn. Leaving 12-inch end, fasten off.

ASSEMBLY

Fold Cap in half. Holding rows 1 and 84 tog, using 12-inch end, **whipstitch edges** *(see illustration)* of Cap tog across to last st, whipstitch twice in last st. Weave rem length through ends of rows around crown of Cap. Pull

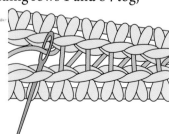

Whipstitch Edges

length tight to gather crown. Fasten off. Turn Cap RS out. Fold Brim up.

LAP ROBE

Row 1: With grey heather, ch 107, sc in 2nd ch from hook and in each rem ch across, turn. *(106 sc)*

Rows 2 & 3: Ch 1, sc in each sc across, turn.

Row 4: Ch 1, sc in first st, dc in next st, *sc in next st, dc in next sc, rep from * across, turn.

Rows 5–9: Rep row 4.

Rows 10–13: [Rep rows 2 and 3 consecutively] twice.

Row 14: Ch 1, sc in each sc across, **changing colors** *(see Stitch Guide)* to black in last sc, turn. Fasten off grey heather.

Row 15: With black, ch 1, sc in each sc across, changing colors to white in last sc, turn. **Do not fasten off** black.

Rows 16 & 17: With white, ch 1, sc in each sc across, turn.

Rows 18 & 19: **Carry black behind** *(see Pattern Notes)*, ch 1, with white, **working over black** *(see Pattern Notes)*, sc in each of first 2 sts, *pick up black, carry white behind, with black, sc in each of next 2 sts, pick up white, carry black behind, sc in each of next 2 sts, rep from * across, turn. Drop white at end of last row.

Rows 20 & 21: With black, ch 1, sc in each sc across, turn.

Rows 22 & 23: Rep rows 18 and 19.

Rows 24 & 25: With white, ch 1, sc in each sc across, turn.

Row 26: Pick up black, with black, ch 1, sc in each sc across, draw up long lp, drop lp from hook, do not turn. Fasten off black.

Row 27: Join grey heather with sc in first sc on last row, sc in each sc across to last sc, sc in last sc and in rem lp from last row, tighten lp.

Rows 28–31: With grey heather, ch 1, sc in each sc across, turn.

Rows 32–38: Ch 1, sc in first st, sc in next st, *sc in next st, dc in next st, rep from * across, turn.

Rows 39–42: Ch 1, sc in each sc across, turn.

Row 43: Ch 1, sc in each sc across, changing colors to black in last sc, turn. Fasten off grey heather.

Rows 44–131: [Rep rows 15–43 consecutively] 3 times, ending last rep at row 41. Fasten off at end of last row.

BORDER

Rnd 1: Join grey heather with sc in any corner, *working in ends of rows across side of Lap Robe, sc in end of each row across to next corner, 3 sc in next corner, sc in each sc across to next corner**, 3 sc in next corner, rep from * around, ending last rep at **, 2 sc in same corner as joining, join with sl st in first sc.

Rnd 2: Ch 1, sl st in each st around, join in first sl st. Fasten off. ∎

Savannah

Aunt died from non-Hodgkin's lymphoma

Star Flower Cap

DESIGN BY **JOYCE BRAGG**

SKILL LEVEL

EASY

FINISHED SIZE
One size fits most

FINISHED MEASUREMENTS
Approx 20-inch circumference

MATERIALS
- NaturallyCaron.com Country medium (worsted) weight yarn (3 oz/185 yds/85g per ball): 1 ball each #0015 deep taupe, #0012 foliage and #0003 soft sunshine
- Sizes G/6/4mm and H/8/5mm crochet hooks or size needed to obtain gauge

GAUGE
Size H hook: 4 hdc = 1 inch; 5 rnds = 2 inches

PATTERN NOTES
Join with slip stitch unless otherwise stated.

Chain-3 at beginning of round counts as first half double crochet unless otherwise stated.

INSTRUCTIONS
CAP
Rnd 1: With size H hook and deep taupe, ch 5, **join** (*see Pattern Notes*) in 5th ch from hook to form a ring, ch 2 (*counts as first hdc*), 9 hdc in ring, join in top of beg ch-2. (*10 sts*)

Rnd 2 & 3: **Ch 3** (*see Pattern Notes*), hdc in same st as beg ch-3, 2 hdc in each rem st around, join in top of beg ch-3. (*40 sts at end of last rnd*)

Rnd 4: Ch 3, hdc in each st around, join in top of beg ch-3.

Rnd 5: Ch 3, hdc in same st as beg ch-3 and in next st, *2 hdc in next st, hdc in next st, rep from * around, join in top of beg ch-3. (*60 sts*)

Rnds 6 & 7: Rep rnd 4.

Rnd 8: Ch 3, hdc in next st, 2 hdc in next st, *hdc in each of next 2 sts, 2 hdc in next st, rep from * around, join in top of beg ch-3. (*80 sts*)

Rnd 9: Rep rnd 4, **changing colors** (*see Stitch Guide*) to soft sunshine at end of rnd.

Rnd 10: With soft sunshine, ch 1, sc in same st as beg ch-1 and in each rem st around, changing colors to deep taupe at end of rnd.

Rnd 11: With deep taupe, rep rnd 4, changing colors to foliage at end of rnd.

Rnd 12: With foliage, rep rnd 10.

Rnds 13–19: Rep rnd 4.

Rnd 20: Change to G hook, ch 1, sc in each st around, join in beg ch-1. Fasten off and weave in ends.

STAR FLOWER
MAKE 1.
Rnd 1: With size H hook and soft sunshine, ch 5, **join** (*see Pattern Notes*) in 5th ch from hook to form ring, ch 6 (*counts as dc and ch-3*), [dc in ring, ch 3] 7 times, join in 3rd ch of beg ch-6.

Rnd 2: Ch 3, [4 dc in next ch-3 sp, dc in next dc] 8 times, join in top of beg ch-3. Fasten off.

Rnd 3: With deep taupe, join in top of beg ch-3 on rnd 2, [ch 6, sc in 2nd ch from hook, hdc in next ch, dc in next ch, tr in next ch, **dtr** (*see Stitch Guide*) in next ch, sk next 4 dc, sc in next dc 2 rows below] 8 times, sc in 3rd ch of beg ch-6 two rows below, join in first st. Fasten off and weave in ends.

Sew points of Star Flower to Cap to attach as shown in photo. ■

Connie

Husband died from cancer 30 years ago

Connie was married to Alvah's son Joe. After Joe passed away, Connie remarried, but she and her husband and all of her children continue to be a part of Alvah's large family that includes 8 children, 19 grandchildren and 29 great-grandchildren.

Alviah

Breast cancer survivor—10 years;
son Joe died 30 years ago
from melanoma

Lots o' Loops Cap

DESIGN BY **MARGARET HUBERT**

SKILL LEVEL

EASY

FINISHED SIZE
One size fits most

FINISHED MEASUREMENTS
Approx 19¼-inch circumference

MATERIALS
- Patons Pure medium (worsted) weight yarn (2¾ oz/117 yds/80g per skein):
    1 skein #20520 ruby rose
- Sizes J/10/6mm and K/10½/6.5mm crochet hooks or size needed to obtain gauge
- Stitch marker

GAUGE
Size K hook: 5 sts = 2 inches

PATTERN NOTES
Do not join unless otherwise stated.

Join with slip stitch unless otherwise stated.

INSTRUCTIONS
CAP
Note: Place a marker at end of rnds 1–5 to mark beg of following rnd. Move marker as each rnd is completed.

Rnd 1: With size K hook, ch 4, **join** (see Pattern Notes) in 4th ch from hook to form ring, 8 sc in ring, join in first sc.

Rnd 2: 2 sc in each sc around, **do not join** (see Pattern Notes). (16 sc)

Rnd 3: *Sc in next sc, 2 sc in next sc, rep from * around, do not join. (24 sc)

Rnd 4: *Sc in each of next 2 sc, 2 sc in next sc, rep from * around, do not join. (32 sc)

Rnd 5: *Sc in each of next 3 sc, 2 sc in next sc, rep from * around, do not join. (40 sc)

Rnd 6: *Sc in each of next 4 sc, 2 sc in next sc, rep from * around, join in first sc. (48 sc)

Rnd 7: Ch 3 (does not count as st), dc in each sc around, join in top of beg ch-3. (48 dc)

Rnd 8: Ch 1, working this rnd in **front lps** (see Stitch Guide), sc in next st, *ch 7**, sc in each of next 2 sc, rep from * ending last rep at **, sc in last sc, join in beg ch-1. (24 ch-7 sps)

Rnd 9: Ch 3, working in **back lps** (see Stitch Guide) of rnd 7, dc in each st around, join in top of beg ch-3. (48 dc)

Rnd 10: Ch 3, working in both lps, dc in each st around, join in top of beg ch-3. (48 dc)

Rnds 11–16: [Rep rnds 8–10 consecutively] twice.

Rnd 17: Rep rnd 8.

Rnd 18: With size J hook, rep rnd 9.

Rnd 19: Ch 1, working through both lps, sc in each st around. Fasten off and weave in ends. ■

Melissa

Diagnosed with breast cancer December 2008;
just completed her treatment

Megan

Donated her hair to Locks of Love

Adult's & Child's
Basket-Weave
Caps

DESIGNS BY **BECKY STEVENS**

ADULT'S CAP

SKILL LEVEL

EASY

FINISHED SIZE
One size fits most

FINISHED MEASUREMENTS
Approx 21-inch circumference

MATERIALS
- Caron Simply Soft medium (worsted) weight yarn (6 oz/315 yds/170g per skein):
    1 skein #9702 off-white
- Size G/6/4mm crochet hook or size needed to obtain gauge

GAUGE
4 sc = 1 inch; 4 sc rows = 1 inch; 7 dc = 2 inches; 5 dc rnds = 2 inches

PATTERN NOTES
Join with slip stitch unless otherwise stated.

Chain-2 at beginning of round counts as first double crochet unless otherwise stated.

SPECIAL STITCHES
Front post double crochet decrease (fpdc dec): Keeping last lp of each fpdc on hook, fpdc around indicated sts, yo, draw lp through all lps on hook.

Back post double crochet decrease (bpdc dec): Keeping last lp of each bpdc on hook, bpdc around indicated sts, yo, draw lp through all lps on hook.

INSTRUCTIONS
RIBBING
Row 1: Ch 9, sc in 2nd ch from hook and each rem ch across, turn. *(8 sc)*

*Note: From this point on, Ribbing rows are worked in **back lps** (see Stitch Guide) unless otherwise stated.*

Rows 2–72: Ch 1, sc in **back lp** *(see Note)* of each st across, turn.

Row 73 (joining row): Working in back lps of previous row and in starting ch on opposite side of row 1, ch 1, sc in each st across, turn. Do not fasten off.

BODY

Rnd 1: Now working in rnds around top of Ribbing, sc in end of each row around, **join** *(see Pattern Notes)* in first sc. *(72 sc)*

Rnd 2: Ch 2 *(see Pattern Notes)*, dc in each st around, join in top of beg ch-2. *(72 sts)*

Rnd 3: Ch 2, **fpdc** *(see Stitch Guide)* around next ch-2, fpdc around each of next 2 dc, ***bpdc** *(see Stitch Guide)* around each of next 3 dc**, fpdc around each of next 3 dc, rep from * around, ending last rep at **, join in top of beg ch-2.

Rnd 4: Ch 2, *fpdc around each of first 3 sts, bpdc around each of next 3 sts, rep from * around, join in top of beg ch-2.

Rnds 5 & 6: Ch 2, bpdc around each of next 3 sts, fpdc around each of next 3 sts, rep from * around, join in top of beg ch-2.

Rnds 7 & 8: Rep rnd 4.

Rnds 9–12: Rep rnds 5–8.

Rnds 13 & 14: Rep rnds 5 and 6.

Rnd 15: Ch 2, ***fpdc dec** *(see Special Stitches)* around first 2 sts, fpdc around next st, work **bpdc dec** *(see Special Stitches)* around next 2 sts, bpdc around next st, rep from * around, join in top of beg ch-2.

Rnd 16: *Fpdc dec around first 2 sts, bpdc dec around next 2 sts, rep from * around, join in top of beg ch-2.

Rnd 17: Ch 2, *fpdc around next st, bpdc around next st, rep from * around, join in top of beg ch-2.

Rnd 18: Ch 2, fpdc around next 2 sts around, join in top of beg ch-2.

Rnd 19: Ch 2, fpdc dec around next 2 sts around, join in top of beg ch-2. Leaving 12-inch length, fasten off.

FINISHING

Weave 12-inch length twice through last rnd of Cap, pull tight. Fasten off and weave in ends.

CHILD'S CAP

SKILL LEVEL

EASY

FINISHED SIZE
One size fits most

FINISHED MEASUREMENTS
Approx 16-inch circumference

MATERIALS
- Caron Simply Soft medium (worsted) weight yarn (6 oz/315 yds/170g per skein):
  1 skein #9702 off-white
- Size G/6/4mm crochet hook or size needed to obtain gauge

GAUGE
4 sc = 1 inch; 4 sc rows = 1 inch; 7 dc = 2 inches; 5 dc rnds = 2 inches

PATTERN NOTES
Join with slip stitch unless otherwise stated.

Chain-2 at beginning of round counts as first double crochet unless otherwise stated.

SPECIAL STITCHES
Front post double crochet decrease (fpdc dec):
Keeping last lp of each fpdc on hook, fpdc around indicated sts, yo, draw lp through all lps on hook.

Back post double crochet decrease (bpdc dec):
Keeping last lp of each bpdc on hook, bpdc around indicated sts, yo, draw lp through all lps on hook.

INSTRUCTIONS
RIBBING
Row 1: Ch 6, sc in 2nd ch from hook and each rem ch across, turn. *(5 sc)*

*Note: From this point on, Ribbing rows are worked in **back lps** (see Stitch Guide) unless otherwise stated.*

Rows 2–54: Ch 1, sc in **back lps** *(see Note)* of each st across, turn.

Row 55 (joining row): Working in back lps of previous row and in starting ch on opposite side of row 1, ch 1, sc in each st across, turn. Do not fasten off.

BODY

Rnd 1: Now working in rnds around top of Ribbing, sc in end of each row around, **join** *(see Pattern Notes)* in first sc. *(54 sc)*

Rnd 2: Ch 2 *(see Pattern Notes)*, dc in each st around, join in top of beg ch-2. *(54 sts)*

Rnd 3: Ch 2, **fpdc** *(see Stitch Guide)* around next ch-2, fpdc around each of next 2 dc, ***bpdc** (see Stitch Guide)* around each of next 3 dc**, fpdc around each of next 3 dc, rep from * around, ending last rep at **, join in top of beg ch-2.

Rnd 4: Ch 2, *fpdc around each of first 3 sts, bpdc around each of next 3 sts, rep from * around, join in top of beg ch-2.

Rnds 5 & 6: Ch 2, bpdc around each of next 3 sts, fpdc around each of next 3 sts, rep from * around, join in top of beg ch-2.

Rnds 7 & 8: Rep rnd 4.

Rnds 9–12: Rep rnds 5–8.

Rnds 13 & 14: Rep rnds 5 and 6.

Rnd 15: Ch 2, ***fpdc dec** (see Special Stitches)* around first 2 sts, fpdc around next st, work **bpdc dec** *(see Special Stitches)* around next 2 sts, bpdc around next st, rep from * around, join in top of beg ch-2.

Rnd 16: *Fpdc dec around first 2 sts, bpdc dec around next 2 sts, rep from * around, join in top of beg ch-2.

Rnd 17: Ch 2, *fpdc around next st, bpdc around next st, rep from * around, join in top of beg ch-2.

Rnd 18: Ch 2, fpdc dec around next 2 sts around, join in top of beg ch-2. Leaving 12-inch length, fasten off.

FINISHING
Weave 12-inch length twice through last rnd of Cap, pull tight. Fasten off and weave in ends. ∎

*M*elissa was Megan's second-grade teacher. That year, Melissa found out she had breast cancer and was not able to finish out the school term. After hearing about Melissa's cancer battle, Megan decided to let her hair grow in order to donate it to Locks of Love, in honor of her teacher. Megan and Melissa still have a close bond.

STITCH GUIDE

FOR MORE COMPLETE INFORMATION,
VISIT **ANNIESCATALOG.COM/STITCHGUIDE**

STITCH ABBREVIATIONS

beg .... begin/begins/beginning
bpdc .... back post double crochet
bpsc ....back post single crochet
bptr ....back post treble crochet
CC .... contrasting color
ch(s) .... chain(s)
ch- .... refers to chain or space
  previously made (i.e., ch-1 space)
ch sp(s) .... chain space(s)
cl(s) .... cluster(s)
cm .... centimeter(s)
dc .... double crochet (singular/plural)
dc dec .... double crochet 2 or more
  stitches together, as indicated
dec .... decrease/decreases/decreasing
dtr .... double treble crochet
ext .... extended
fpdc .... front post double crochet
fpsc .... front post single crochet
fptr .... front post treble crochet
g .... gram(s)
hdc .... half double crochet
hdc dec .... half double crochet 2 or more
  stitches together, as indicated
inc .... increase/increases/increasing
lp(s) .... loop(s)
MC .... main color
mm .... millimeter(s)
oz .... ounce(s)
pc .... popcorn(s)
rem .... remain/remains/remaining
rep(s) .... repeat(s)
rnd(s) .... round(s)
RS .... right side
sc .... single crochet (singular/plural)
sc dec ....single crochet 2 or more
  stitches together, as indicated
sk .... skip/skipped/skipping
sl st(s) .... slip stitch(es)
sp(s) .... space(s)/spaced
st(s) .... stitch(es)
tog .... together
tr .... treble crochet
trtr .... triple treble
WS .... wrong side
yd(s) .... yard(s)
yo .... yarn over

YARN CONVERSION

OUNCES TO GRAMS		GRAMS TO OUNCES	
1	28.4	25	⅞
2	56.7	40	1⅔
3	85.0	50	1¾
4	113.4	100	3½

UNITED STATES		UNITED KINGDOM
sl st (slip stitch)	=	sc (single crochet)
sc (single crochet)	=	dc (double crochet)
hdc (half double crochet)	=	htr (half treble crochet)
dc (double crochet)	=	tr (treble crochet)
tr (treble crochet)	=	dtr (double treble crochet)
dtr (double treble crochet)	=	ttr (triple treble crochet)
skip	=	miss

Reverse single crochet (reverse sc): Ch 1, sk first st, working from left to right, insert hook in next st from front to back, draw up lp on hook, yo and draw through both lps on hook.

Chain (ch): Yo, pull through lp on hook.

Single crochet (sc): Insert hook in st, yo, pull through st, yo, pull through both lps on hook.

Double crochet (dc): Yo, insert hook in st, yo, pull through st, [yo, pull through 2 lps] twice.

Front loop (front lp) Back loop (back lp)

Front Loop   Back Loop

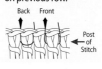

Front post stitch (fp): Back post stitch (bp): When working post st, insert hook from right to left around post of st on previous row.

Back   Front

Post of Stitch

Half double crochet (hdc): Yo, insert hook in st, yo, pull through st, yo, pull through all 3 lps on hook.

Double treble crochet (dtr): Yo 3 times, insert hook in st, yo, pull through st, [yo, pull through 2 lps] 4 times.

Slip stitch (sl st): Insert hook in st, pull through both lps on hook.

Chain color change (ch color change) Yo with new color, draw through last lp on hook.

Double crochet color change (dc color change) Drop first color, yo with new color, draw through last 2 lps of st.

Treble crochet (tr): Yo twice, insert hook in st, yo, pull through st, [yo, pull through 2 lps] 3 times.

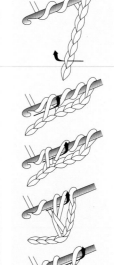

Single crochet decrease (sc dec): (Insert hook, yo, draw lp through) in each of the sts indicated, yo, draw through all lps on hook.

Example of 2-sc dec

Half double crochet decrease (hdc dec): (Yo, insert hook, yo, draw lp through) in each of the sts indicated, yo, draw through all lps on hook.

Example of 2-hdc dec

Double crochet decrease (dc dec): (Yo, insert hook, yo, draw lp through, yo, draw through 2 lps on hook) in each of the sts indicated, yo, draw through all lps on hook.

Example of 2-dc dec

Treble crochet decrease (tr dec): Holding back last lp of each st, tr in each of the sts indicated, yo, pull through all lps on hook.

Example of 2-tr dec

Metric
Conversion
Charts

METRIC CONVERSIONS

yards	x	.9144	=	metres (m)
yards	x	91.44	=	centimetres (cm)
inches	x	2.54	=	centimetres (cm)
inches	x	25.40	=	millimetres (mm)
inches	x	.0254	=	metres (m)

centimetres	x	.3937	=	inches
metres	x	1.0936	=	yards

INCHES INTO MILLIMETRES & CENTIMETRES (Rounded off slightly)

inches	mm	cm	inches	cm	inches	cm	inches	cm
1/8	3	0.3	5	12.5	21	53.5	38	96.5
1/4	6	0.6	5 1/2	14	22	56	39	99
3/8	10	1	6	15	23	58.5	40	101.5
1/2	13	1.3	7	18	24	61	41	104
5/8	15	1.5	8	20.5	25	63.5	42	106.5
3/4	20	2	9	23	26	66	43	109
7/8	22	2.2	10	25.5	27	68.5	44	112
1	25	2.5	11	28	28	71	45	114.5
1 1/4	32	3.2	12	30.5	29	73.5	46	117
1 1/2	38	3.8	13	33	30	76	47	119.5
1 3/4	45	4.5	14	35.5	31	79	48	122
2	50	5	15	38	32	81.5	49	124.5
2 1/2	65	6.5	16	40.5	33	84	50	127
3	75	7.5	17	43	34	86.5		
3 1/2	90	9	18	46	35	89		
4	100	10	19	48.5	36	91.5		
4 1/2	115	11.5	20	51	37	94		

KNITTING NEEDLES CONVERSION CHART

Canada/U.S.	0	1	2	3	4	5	6	7	8	9	10	10½	11	13	15
Metric (mm)	2	2¼	2¾	3¼	3½	3¾	4	4½	5	5½	6	6½	8	9	10

CROCHET HOOKS CONVERSION CHART

Canada/U.S.	1/B	2/C	3/D	4/E	5/F	6/G	8/H	9/I	10/J	10½/K	N
Metric (mm)	2.25	2.75	3.25	3.5	3.75	4.25	5	5.5	6	6.5	9.0

Annie's®

Chemo Caps & Wraps is published by Annie's, 306 East Parr Road, Berne, IN 46711. Printed in USA. Copyright © 2010, 2013 Annie's. All rights reserved. This publication may not be reproduced in part or in whole without written permission from the publisher.

RETAIL STORES: If you would like to carry this pattern book or any other Annie's publication, visit AnniesWSL.com

Every effort has been made to ensure that the instructions in this pattern book are complete and accurate. We cannot, however, take responsibility for human error, typographical mistakes or variations in individual work. Please visit AnniesCustomerCare.com to check for pattern updates.

ISBN: 978-1-59635-327-5
10 11 12 13 14